WORD PICTURES PAINTED BY PAUL

Word Pictures

PAINTED
BY PAUL

SANDY PETRO

VICTOR BOOKS

A DIVISION OF SCRIPTURE PRESS PUBLICATIONS INC.
USA CANADA ENGLAND

Scripture quotations are from the *Holy Bible, New International Version*®. Copyright © 1973, 1978, 1984 by International Bible Society. Used by permission of Zondervan Publishing House. All rights reserved. Scripture quotations marked (NASB) are from the *New American Standard Bible*, © the Lockman Foundation 1960, 1962, 1963, 1968, 1971, 1972, 1973, 1975, 1977. Scripture quotations marked (AMP) are taken from *The Amplified New Testament*, © 1954, 1958 the Lockman Foundation.

Editors: Carolyn Nystrom and Patricia Picardi
Cover Design: Larry Taylor
Cover Illustration: Joe VanSeveren

Recommended Dewey Decimal Classification: 227.3
Suggested Subject Heading: BIBLE, N.T., 2 CORINTHIANS, METAPHOR

Library of Congress Catalog Card Number: 93-16024
ISBN: 1-56476-034-0

1 2 3 4 5 6 7 8 9 10 Printing/Year 97 96 95 94 93

VICTOR BOOKS
A division of SP Publications, Inc.
Wheaton, Illinois 60187

CONTENTS

In one ear and out the other. How many times have your *important* words taken this route? How did you feel? Frustrated? Disappointed? Angry? Can you imagine God's dismay if His Word—which He commands us to treasure in our hearts (Proverbs 2:1)—were to follow the same course? But God, in His great wisdom, has taken precautions to prevent this from happening.

Regardless of how hard we try, we often fail to communicate in a *meaningful* way, but God never does! "All Scripture is God-breathed and is useful for teaching, rebuking, correcting and training in righteousness, so that the man of God may be thoroughly equipped for every good work" (2 Timothy 3:16). Throughout the Bible we see a communication tool that *captures our attention, makes the truth of God's Word unforgettable, and draws us into intimacy with Himself.* Even Jesus used this tool as a primary method of teaching, challenging, and motivating others. It is known as "word pictures."

Gary Smalley and John Trent in their book, *The Language of Love,* define a word picture as: "a communication tool that uses a story or an object to activate simultaneously the emotions and intellect of a person. In doing so, it causes a person to experience our words, not just hear them."

By focusing on *the familiar,* word pictures in the Bible allow us to experience God's Word in a way that can bring spiritual growth and new meaning to our lives.

Word Pictures Painted by Paul focuses on Paul's second letter to the Corinthian church. In 2 Corinthians, Paul places the Corinthian church on his easel and boldly strokes the canvas of the Corinthian hearts and minds with eight word pictures created from the palette of God's truth! Paul paints clay pots hiding infinite treasure, and we recognize ourselves as mundane creatures housing the holy Christ. Paul paints a thorn rammed into delicate flesh, and we wince away from our own inescapable jabs of pain. Paul paints the human body as a flimsy tent, and we groan with longing for new bodies—fit for heaven.

8

Examining the Background

Ominous dangers threatened the Corinthian church. Paul knew that he must act quickly and forcefully to protect this beloved church which he had organized during his second missionary journey. Even though Paul had written a first letter of instruction, false teachers had infiltrated the church. These false teachers hoped to throw Paul's personal integrity and authority as an apostle into question. So Paul wrote a second time. This time, Paul knew that he had to make every word count. He needed a means of communication that would *grab the Corinthians' attention, impact their lives, and lock his message in their minds.* So Paul used word pictures to maximize insight and understanding so that the Corinthians could reject all false teaching and mature in Christ, by becoming steadfast in faith.

How exciting that these word pictures can do as much, if not more, for us than they did for the Corinthians! As Paul's word pictures penetrate your heart and mind, you will find essential spiritual truths concerning relationships, giving, death, humility, dependency upon God—His Gospel, and His grace actively expressing themselves in your life!

Using this Guide

Each chapter of this study is divided into five sections:

☐ *Gathering Information* is designed to help you discover what the Scripture passage is saying. Thought-provoking questions will help uncover background information needed to understand the passage, interpret God's Word, and apply it to your life.

☐ *Gaining Insight* expands on the theme and spiritual concepts found in the first section enhancing your understanding of God's Word.

☐ *Getting Involved* challenges you to action! In this section you will learn to apply God's Word to your life by keeping a *Life Action Diary*. This diary is composed of two sections. Each day of the week you will read an assigned portion of Scripture, asking the Lord: "How can this apply to my life?" Then in one or two sentences, you will write your answer to that question under *Application*. Next, as you meditate on your written application, ask the Lord: "What can I do today to put this truth into action?" Write what you have purposed to do under the *Action* section. Here is an example of how to keep your life action diary.

Monday: Read James 3:1-12.

Application: Lord, I am guilty of having a sharp tongue at times. Forgive me when my words have hurt others as well as You.

Action: Today I will pay special attention to my words, using them to build others up and not tear them down. I will, if necessary, pray before I speak, so that I may better control my tongue.

Tuesday: Read Psalm 139:13-16.

Application: Many times I have a hard time believing I am actually "fearfully and wonderfully" made. There are so many things that make me dissatisfied with myself.

Action: Today I will choose to believe what God's Word says about me. I will make a list of my positive qualities and spend time praising God for who I am and how He has made me.

☐ *Growing Intimate* focuses on prayer as you grow closer both with group members and with the Lord. There are also two parts to this section. In the first part, "Partners in Prayer," you can record prayer requests for the individuals in your Bible study group. Try to pray daily for the needs of these friends (in accordance with Galatians 6:1). The second part, "Pen and Paper Prayers," provides opportunity to develop a well-rounded prayer life by writing a prayer that includes the following elements:

Adoration—worship your Lord! Freely express your love for Him, concentrating on who He is.

Confession—confess any sins in your life. Include sins of omission as well as commission.

Petition—make your personal needs known to God.

Intercession—pray for friends, family, pastors, neighbors, employers, fellow employees.

Thanksgiving—praise God for what He has done and what He will do!

Write your "Pen and Paper Prayer" after you complete the *Gathering Information* and *Gaining Insight* sections, so that your prayer focuses on the spiritual truths and theme of each lesson.

Word Pictures Painted by Paul can be used in your own personal Bible study. It will also work as a group study.

☐ *Guiding Interaction* is an aid for anyone desiring to lead a group through this study. It provides discussion questions that will allow people in a group to respond together to what they are learning through personal study of the front section of the book. Even if not everyone in the group completes the personal study sections of the book, these discussion questions will provide an outline for group members to nurture one another through a shared study of God's Word.

As you work through this book and the word pictures of 2 Corinthians, I challenge you to put yourself on Paul's easel and allow him to brighten your life with the dynamic splashes of colorful truth found in God's Word!

THE FRAGRANCE OF

Life and Death

❧ GATHERING INFORMATION ❧

1. What are two or three of your favorite smells? Why are you drawn to them?

Think of some smells that repel you and explain why.

Do you wear perfume? Why or why not?

From your answers above, what general patterns do you see in your personal reactions to the sense of smell?

Read 2 Corinthians 2:14-17.
2. What "fragrance" do Paul and the Corinthians wear?

Describe the qualities of the aroma that would make that fragrance noticeable to others.

What positive and negative examples from your own everyday life illustrate how the fragrance Paul describes gets noticed by others?

3. The following Scripture passages describe fundamental truths about God's "aroma," the Gospel. Briefly summarize each of them.

1 Corinthians 15:1-6

John 3:3-7

Colossians 1:21-23

Colossians 2:6-7

4. In view of the biblical teachings thus far in this study, are you wearing the fragrance of Christ? How can you tell?

5. Ecclesiastes 10:1 says: "Dead flies make a perfumer's oil stink." What "dead flies" spoil the fragrance of Christ in your life? What can you do to get rid of these "flies"?

6. According to 2 Corinthians 2:15-16, in what two ways do people react when they are exposed to the fragrance of Christ?

   What explanation does Paul offer for why the same fragrance causes such different responses?

7. What do the following verses reveal about "salvation"?

   Ephesians 2:8-10

   John 3:16-21

   Acts 16:29-31

   1 Timothy 2:1-6

12

In Paul's word picture about the fragrance of Christ (1 Corinthians 2) he wrote that God's people are the aroma of Christ among those who are being saved. In view of the above texts, explain in your own words *what* it means to be saved, *how* we can be saved, and *who* can be saved.

what:

how:

who:

Do you ever doubt your salvation? Spend some time reading through the Book of 1 John. Based on what John says in 5:1-13, what indications can you look for to assure you that you belong to God?

8. In Paul's word picture of fragrance, he spoke of people who are being saved but he also spoke of those who are "perishing." What do the following verses teach about those who are perishing?

Psalm 73:27

Revelation 20:11-15

2 Peter 3:8-9

According to the above texts, who will perish? Where will they go? How can we avoid this judgment?

Who do you know that you fear is perishing? Commit yourself to pray regularly for his or her salvation.

9. According to 1 Corinthians 15:9-10 and Ephesians 2:8-9, God's grace equips us to serve Him. What then is the answer to Paul's question in 2 Corinthians 2:16 about "who is equal to such a task"?

Under what circumstances do you feel inadequate to serve God?

What can you do to trust Him more with these circumstances?

In Paul's day, as in ours, there were some who were "peddling" ("corrupting," KJV) the Word of God for profit (2 Corinthians 2:17). What does it mean to "peddle" the Gospel, and what examples do you see of Gospel-peddling today?

10. According to 2 Corinthians 2:17, what character quality must a genuine representative of Christ have?

Why do you think this quality is important?

In 2 Corinthians 1:12, what characteristic does the Bible combine with sincerity? Why do the two go together?

Note: In the KJV, the NASB, and the NIV versions of the Bible, the words "sincere" and "pure" are often interchanged. An example would be Philippians 1:10 where sincere is used in the KJV and NASB but is replaced with pure in the NIV.
In 2 Peter 3:1, Peter says that he writes the believers in order to stir up a "sincere mind" according to NASB, a "pure mind" in KJV, and "wholesome thinking" in the words of NIV. How, according to 2 Peter 3:2, can we develop this kind of sincerity?

What are some ways you can practice this sincerity in your own life?

❧ GAINING INSIGHT ❧

"Mom, it smells like Sandy in here," Jeff said.
My friend Marilyn and her son Jeff were walking through the cosmetic section in a department store. As Marilyn looked around, a display of "Ruffles" perfume, body lotion, and bath oil beads caught her attention.

"You're right, Jeff," Marilyn laughed. "We're standing next to the only fragrance Sandy ever wears."

When Marilyn told me the story later I had to smile, realizing for the first time that I had a trademark. I wondered how many other people associated me with Ruffles perfume. It was fun having a fragrance I could call my own.

Paul's words in 2 Corinthians 2:14-17 make me hope that I am recognized for wearing another more important fragrance—the aroma of Christ. In these verses Paul paints a word picture, portraying the Corinthian believers as being like a perfume that others can't help noticing. He describes the *aroma* and *appeal* of the fragrance of Christ and then discusses the *adequacy* and *approach* of those who wear it.

There is a more subtle word picture in verse 14 which strengthens his portrayal of the fragrant Christian. The NIV most clearly depicts this image: "But thanks be to God, who always leads us in a triumphal procession in Christ and through us spreads everywhere the fragrance of the knowledge of Him." Here the imagery may be an allusion to the Roman practice where the triumphant Roman general paraded his soldiers and the captives through the streets of Rome. Marching along with them were priests swinging large censers that burned sweet-smelling incense. Although the incense was offered as a sacrifice to the gods, it carried a clear message to the people. To the victors, the aroma was the sweet scent of a victorious life. To the captives it was a reminder of their imminent death.

We Christians are like soldiers who serve the Lord Jesus Christ

(2 Timothy 2:3). We are called to engage in spiritual warfare (Ephesians 6:10-18), knowing we will be led to victory by God in Christ. How wonderful that Christ at the cross triumphed over sin and death, so that we, when we accept Him as our personal Savior, can share in that triumph! Then, God, through the power of the Holy Spirit within us, spreads the sweet *aroma* of the knowledge of Christ to the world through us.

Have you ever realized that as we distribute the fragrance of the Gospel message through our actions and words, we are really offering ourselves to God as living sacrifices? (Romans 12:1-2) Our Gospel aroma is always pleasing and acceptable in God's sight. I'm afraid, however, that it is not always as well received by the people around us. Verse 16 confirms that the *appeal* of the Gospel will vary. Please understand that the aroma of the Gospel never changes; it is always sweet smelling. It is just received differently by different people. To those being saved (the victors), it is the smell of life—abundant and eternal. To those who are perishing (the captives), it is the smell of death—their own death to which they are doomed because they have rejected God's grace.

I have seen these contrasting responses to the Gospel in my visits to prisons. Whenever I serve as Coordinator for the Bill Glass Prison Ministry, I enter a prison with other counselors to share the Gospel message with anyone who desires to listen. Over a period of three days, we have contact with a large percentage of the prison population. Many inmates are attracted to us just as a bee is drawn to the sweet smell of nectar. Others, however, avoid us and our aroma completely.

Have you ever felt inadequate to be a representative of Christ and His Gospel? I have. It is a heavy responsibility. Even Paul, one of the most effective evangelists ever, raises the question of *adequacy* in 2 Corinthians 2:16. But a page later he encourages us in 2 Corinthians 3:5 with the reminder that our competency comes from God. I see three phrases in 2 Corinthians 2:17 that can build our confidence and help us feel more adequate.

First, we, like Paul, have been "sent from God." As His disciples, we are divinely commissioned to go into the world and share His Gospel (Matthew 28:18-20). Second, "in Christ we speak." Christ gives us divine authority and power through the Holy Spirit when we speak of Him to others (1 Thessalonians 1:5). As Christ's ambassadors, God equips us to proclaim His Gospel just as He did Paul and the Corinthians. Third, we speak "before God." That is, we speak in the sight of God. We can take courage that when we share His Gospel, He is right there beside us, guiding us as we speak (Luke 21:15).

As you carry out your commission in the sight of God, be aware that you are accountable to God for what you do and say (2 Corinthians 5:10). Second Corinthians 2:17 reminds us that we must not only "adequately" represent God, we must also "accurately" represent Him. Paul calls attention to those in the church who handle the Word of God like a salesman who peddles his wares and is only interested in making money—not in serving the customer. It is interesting that as I write this chapter, the news media, only a few weeks ago, presented a documentary on three well-known TV evangelists. The documentary portrayed these evangelists as fraudulent hucksters. The media's evidence indicated that each man had adulterated truth in order to gain a selfish advantage of millions of dollars. Yet from 2 Corinthians 2:17, I understand that the key ingredient for any representative of God must be sincerity. As we *approach* others for Christ, we must be careful to maintain sincerity in both motive and message.

So, fragrance-bearer, be ever mindful of your *approach*, depend on Christ for your *adequacy*, and be prepared to encounter differences in the Gospel's *appeal*. I pray that each time you apply your favorite perfume, its fragrance will remind you of the even more wonderful *aroma* that you wear through Christ Jesus.

❦ GETTING INVOLVED ❦

Today you will begin keeping your *Life Action Diary*. Be sure you have read the *Introduction* on page 8 which explains how to journal. The following Scripture passages are meant to help you to daily spread the fragrance of Christ to others.

SUNDAY: Read Colossians 4:2-6.
Application:

Action:

MONDAY: Read Ephesians 6:10-20.
Application:

Action:

TUESDAY: Read 1 Peter 3:1-5.
Application:

Action:

WEDNESDAY: Read 1 Peter 2:1-3 and 2 Timothy 2:15.
Application:

Action:

THURSDAY: Read Matthew 5:1-12.
Application:

Action:

FRIDAY: Read Matthew 5:13-16.
Application:

Action:

SATURDAY: Read 2 Timothy 1:7 and Romans 1:16.
Application:

Action:

❦ *GROWING INTIMATE* ❦

Partners in Prayer (Record prayer requests for group members)

Pen and Paper Prayer (Write your own prayer following the instructions given in the *Introduction* on page 9.)

CHAPTER TWO

LETTERS WRITTEN ON

Human Hearts

❦ GATHERING INFORMATION ❦

1. Have you ever needed a letter of recommendation? What was the circumstance?

2. Read the following examples in Scripture where people were commended by letters. Then complete the chart below.

	Who was being recommended?	*Who was writing the recommendation?*
Acts 18:24-28		
Romans 16:1-2		
2 Corinthians 8:16-24		

Considering the Scripture references you just read, why do you think the custom of sending letters of recommendation developed in the early days of the church? Why was it valuable?

Read 2 Corinthians 3:1-6.

3. Based on the information in your chart (question 2), do you think Paul was for or against using letters of recommendation? Why in 2 Corinthians 3:1 does Paul seem to belittle his need for a letter of recommendation?

What information might you draw from 1 Corinthians 9:1-2 to explain Paul's feelings about letters of recommendation for himself?

4. Look again at 2 Corinthians 3:1-6. In what ways were the Corinthians "living letters" for Paul? For Christ?

Why do you think Paul used the word picture of a letter to refer to people?

For whom are you a living letter?

What do you think people read in the letter of your life?

What would you like them to read?

How can you accomplish this?

5. Who is the author of the living letters in Paul's word picture? What was Paul's responsibility regarding the development of these letters?

6. Read Exodus 24:12; 31:18; and 32:15-16. What was written on the tablets of stone, and who did the writing?

7. Read the following Scriptures. Who does the writing on human hearts, and what are the results?

John 3:3-6

2 Corinthians 5:17

Hebrews 8:10-12

Have you personally experienced these results? When and how have you seen this kind of evidence that God is writing His letter on your own life?

8. Reread 2 Corinthians 3:4-6. What is the origin of Paul's confidence? What is the basis of his adequacy?

How consistent are you at placing your confidence and competency in the same source that Paul does? What factors cause you to succeed? To fail?

9. Paul says in 2 Corinthians 3:6 that we are competent as ministers of a New Covenant. Read Hebrews 9:11-23. Briefly explain the New Covenant.

Who, according to 2 Corinthians 5:17-21, does God make competent to be ministers of the New Covenant?

According to 1 Timothy 4:6-16, what are some of the responsibilities of God's servants?

In view of these texts, evaluate yourself as a minister of the New Covenant. What improvements do you want to make?

10. According to 2 Corinthians 3:6, what is the main contrast between the Old and the New Covenant?

Read the following passages and write the main differences between the Old Covenant and the New.

Romans 7:4-13

Galatians 3:19-29

Hebrews 9:8-15

11. Look again at 2 Corinthians 3:6. Are you living according to the Law or according to the Spirit? Give some examples to explain your answer.

12. Verse 6 in the NASB speaks of us as "servants of a New Covenant." In view of your study of these texts, what would you say it means to be a "servant of the New Covenant"?

Who do you know who is characterized by their servanthood to God? What is it about that person that you admire?

13. How would you like to better express the letter Christ is writing on your heart?

For Extra Challenge
Question 10 considers differences between the Old and New Covenant. For a more in-depth understanding, read the following Scriptures and explain how the Law kills, but the Spirit gives life.

Ezekiel 36:26-27
John 6:63
Romans 5:12-13
Romans 6:23
Galatians 3:11
Titus 3:5-6
1 Peter 3:18
1 John 5:11-13

What can the passages above add to your understanding of Paul's word picture of letters on the heart in 2 Corinthians 3:1-6?

❦ GAINING INSIGHT ❦

For years the house down the road had caught my attention. Because of its location I had to pass it whenever I went anywhere. The house intrigued me because, while its structure was appealing, its appearance was appalling! The paint was faded and peeling, shutters and shingles were missing, windows were cracked, the lawn had died out, trash cluttered the lawn, and there was no sign of landscaping.

But one day I began to notice drastic changes taking place. Within a month the house had new paint, windows, and shutters. The roof had been repaired, the lawn replanted, and attractive landscaping added. Everything about the house became immaculate. It was clear that either the house had new owners or the old owners had adopted new incentives and values.

I envision the changes in the lives of the Corinthian believers to be as phenomenal as the renovations in that house. As the Holy Spirit came and took up residence in Corinthian hearts, He gave them new incentives and values. These resulted in life-changes that were easily recognized by those around them.

Paul emphasizes these changes in 2 Corinthians 3:1-6 by using the metaphor of letter writing. He paints for us a word picture by declaring that the Corinthian believers were *living, legible,* and *lasting* letters, not only for Christ but for himself. Just think, the Corinthian church had once lived as pagans, but now they were living as Christians! The message of the Gospel and the power of Christ were plainly written upon the lives of the Corinthians so that everyone could read.

These public living letters were penned by Christ through the grace of God, but they were delivered by Paul through his ministry to them. Therefore, the existence of the Corinthian church was a testimonial for the authority of Paul's apostleship. Although it was customary for apostles to carry letters of recommendation attesting to their character and authority, the very lives of the Corinthians, living as men and women in

Christ, were the best and only letter Paul needed.

These "unique" credentials of Paul's were superior to his opponents, not only because they could be read by everyone, but also because of their permanence. Paul's opponents carried letters written with ink which could fade or be deleted. But Paul's living letters, instead of being written with fallible man-made products, were written with the infallible Spirit of the living God.

Did you know that just as God Himself, wrote His law on the tablets of stone for Moses and the Israelites, God Himself writes His message of hope on softened hearts today? When we accept Christ as our personal Savior, we (like the Corinthians) become living letters — signed by Christ and sealed by the Holy Spirit (Ephesians 1:13-14). Christ erases our previously filled pages of sin and begins to fill the new pages of our lives with His Words and His handwriting.

Charles Swindoll says:

> Like handwriting on a page, Jesus fills us. Although people cannot see the Author, they can see His words and feel their impact. They can touch the pages of our lives and feel His heartbeat — His presence. As living letters, we reflect the Lord — from the truth of the words to the grace of the penmanship.[1]
>
> By reading our lives, people form their opinions about Christ and Christianity. Christ will either be cherished or crumpled up and thrown into the trash. We are mailed as an authorized representative of Christ, and it is essential that we carry His authentic message of love for them to read.
>
> How about your living letter? Is it warm and inviting or cold and impersonal? Are you sending out junk mail that no one is bothering to read, or do those around you eagerly await your delivery? Maybe you just need some fresh stationery and some time alone with Jesus, allowing Him to do the revising.[2]

In 2 Corinthians 3:1-6, Paul challenges those who have experienced the work of the Holy Spirit not only to be quality letters for Christ, but to create new human living letters for Him. We are to do this in the same manner as Paul, who was equipped with confidence and competency from God to carry the message of the New Covenant of grace.

What is the message of the New Covenant? For a fuller understanding, we need to see the New Covenant in light of the Old (2 Corinthians 3:6). The New Covenant, which is based on the work of the Holy Spirit, leads to life. The Old Covenant, which was based on obedience to a code of laws, brought the awareness of sin and death (Romans 5:12-21).

What about you? Are you living your life under the bondage of the Old Covenant or under the freedom of the New Covenant? I believe that many people in our churches are in bondage to the law of the Old Covenant without even realizing it. I speak from experience.

For many years I sat in church seeking heaven through my own efforts instead of depending upon the grace of God. I began attending church regularly in high school, but it was not until I was in my early twenties that I heard and acted upon the New Covenant message.

During a special weekend program at my church, I was asked two questions that helped change my life. I was first asked that if I were to die that day, did I know for sure that I would go to heaven?[3] My answer was, "No." In trying to evaluate my behavior, I decided that even though I wasn't a terrible person, I had probably been bad enough not to make it in.

I was then asked that if I were to die and stand before God, and He were to ask me why He should let me into His heaven, what would I say?[4] My response included the facts that I attended church regularly, I tried to be a good person, and I was a Sunday School teacher and a committee worker.

It was then that I heard for the first time that eternal life was a free gift. Heaven was not something I could earn or deserve by the things that I did. I was told that I could receive eternal life just by praying a simple prayer of faith.

Prior to that weekend, I had a *head* knowledge of Christ, but finally I understood with my *heart* what Christ had done for me. I had always known that Christ died for the sins of mankind, but through my head knowledge, I saw myself as a blurred part of a large crowd. My new heart knowledge was making me realize that Jesus died for my individual sins—in a very personal way. I finally understood that through His death, burial, and resurrection (three days later) Christ was offering to me, Sandy Petro, abundant living here on earth as well as life forever with Him in heaven. All I had to do was recognize that I was a sinner, pray asking God to forgive my sins, and ask Christ to come into my life as my personal Savior.

That is exactly what I did in February 1972. It was then that I became a living letter for Christ, as His Spirit placed the seal of His handwriting on my heart.

Have you delivered God's message of forgiveness and eternal life through Christ to anyone lately? 2 Corinthians 5:18-20 says:

All this is from God, who reconciled us to himself through Christ and gave us the ministry of reconciliation: that God was reconciling the world to himself in Christ, not counting men's sins against them. And he has committed to us the message of reconciliation. We are therefore Christ's ambassadors, as though God were making his appeal through us. We implore you on Christ's behalf: Be reconciled to God.

In whom do you place your confidence and competence for such a task—yourself or Christ? If opponents questioned your credentials as a minister of the Gospel message, what evidence could you offer them? I pray that you, like Paul, will have *living, legible,* and *lasting* letters of recommendation written on tablets of human hearts!

❦ *GETTING INVOLVED* ❦

Continue keeping your *Life Action Diary*. The following Scripture passages will help you focus on your role as a living letter for Christ and on your responsibility of creating new living letters.

SUNDAY: Read Colossians 1:9-12.
Application:

Action:

MONDAY: Read Colossians 3:1-11.
Application:

Action:

TUESDAY: Read Colossians 3:12-17.
Application:

Action:

WEDNESDAY: Read Ephesians 4:17-28.
Application:

Action:

THURSDAY: Read Ephesians 4:29-32.
Application:

Action:

FRIDAY: Read Galatians 5:16-26.
Application:

Action:

SATURDAY: Read 2 Corinthians 5:17-21.
Application:

Action:

❦ *GROWING INTIMATE* ❦

Partners in Prayer (Record prayer needs of group members.)

Pen and Paper Prayer (Write your own prayer following the instructions given in the Introduction.)

CHAPTER THREE

VEILED AND UNVEILED

❦GATHERING INFORMATION❦

1. Have you ever had a useful or treasured possession that, after serving its purpose, you replaced it with something that turned out to be even better than the original? Explain briefly. Include statements concerning your feelings about the "old" and the "new."

Read Exodus 34:27-35.

2. What difference could the Israelites see in Moses as he descended from Mount Sinai with the Ten Commandments? What caused this difference?

When have you experienced something so dramatic that it left you visibly changed? Describe the change.

How did Aaron and the Israelites respond to what they saw?

When did Moses veil and unveil his face?

Why do you think he covered and uncovered his face at these times?

What things in our lives could cause God's radiance within us to fade? To increase?

Are there situations today in which a Christian should "veil" her

31

relationship with the Lord? Explain.

Read 2 Corinthians 3:7-18.
3. Why, according to Paul, did Moses veil his face?

What do these verses reveal the radiance of Moses' face to be?

Verse 14 speaks of the Old Covenant. How does Moses' reason for covering his face relate to the Old Covenant?

Many texts of Scripture speak of God's glory. *Describe* the "glory of the Lord" according to Revelation 21:9-11, 22-27.

Who radiates the glory of the Lord according to Hebrews 1:1-3 and 2 Corinthians 3:18?

How do we share in the glory of the Lord according to:

2 Corinthians 3:18

2 Corinthians 4:5-7

Romans 8:17

John 15:5-8

John 17:22-23

In view of these texts, list specific ways that you can reflect God's glory to others.

Considering God's glory as you have studied it thus far, would you say that you reflect Him like a spotless mirror or one with smudges? Explain.

How could 1 John 1:9 help you?

4. Reread 2 Corinthians 3:7-11. Note how Paul uses the word "ministry" to refer to both the New and Old Covenants. What three sets of
opposites summarize how the glory of the New Covenant surpasses
the glory of the Old Covenant?

	Old	**New**
(a)		
(b)		
(c)		

How would you describe the superiority of the New Covenant?

Read Hebrews 10:1-18. Which verses here help explain the three
superior characteristics of the New Covenant? How?

Read Mark 15:38 and Hebrews 10:19-23. How do these verses
further reveal the superiority of the New Covenant?

5. What is the "hope" Paul talks about in 2 Corinthians 3:12? Who has
this hope? (See also 1 Thessalonians 5:8-11 and Titus 3:7.)

Paul says in 2 Corinthians 3:12 that this hope makes us bold. Why?

In what circumstances do you think that this hope should cause
boldness?

Read 2 Corinthians 4:1-6.
6. Review 2 Corinthians 3:12-18. In your own words explain what you
think Paul means by a "veiled heart," a "veiled mind," and a "veiled
Gospel."

How would you relate 1 Corinthians 1:18; Hebrews 3:12-13; and

Romans 8:5-8 to your conclusions in the previous question?

Do you know anyone with a veiled heart or mind? Pause right now to pray for that person. Ask that the light of Christ would transform his or her darkness.

7. Explain how Romans 10:8-13 relates to 2 Corinthians 3:16. Describe when and how your own "veil" was removed?

8. 2 Corinthians 3:17 talks about our freedom in Christ. Read Romans 6:17-18 and 22-23. What do these verses say about what we have been "freed" from, and what we are "freed" to do?

9. According to 2 Corinthians 4:1-6, how does a person become a minister of the New Covenant? How does this apply to you personally?

What qualifications, according to this text, should a minister of the New Covenant have?

How do you measure up? What are your strengths? Your weaknesses?

What steps could you take to strengthen your weaknesses?

10. Paul speaks in 2 Corinthians 4:4 of the "god of this age." Why do you think that Paul refers to Satan with this title?

What are some ways that Satan uses today to keep people veiled from the truth of Christ?

What areas of your own life do you sometimes try to veil from the light of God's Word?

How can 1 John 1:8-9 help you surrender these areas to the Lord?

❧ GAINING INSIGHT ❧

One Christmas I eagerly unwrapped the gift my husband placed before me, having no idea what it might be. Inside a big box was cradled a smaller one. I gasped with surprise as I gazed down at the beautiful new wedding ring inside. The beauty of it clearly surpassed the ring that I wore on my left hand, but it wasn't the appearance of the ring I cared about. My heart leaped with joy over the unspoken but clearly understood words expressed by the special gift.

The new ring represented the new beginning Joe and I were experiencing in our twelve-year-old marriage. We had come through hard times. We began our marriage unaware of what it meant to have a personal relationship with Christ. Then, when I came to know Christ before Joe, we struggled through a time of being unequally yoked. We had for the past year, however (since Joe had accepted Christ as his personal Savior), been living under a new covenant, a new agreement. Our relationship was now guided by God's Word, and we had a new power through the Holy Spirit to enable our marriage to survive. Things weren't perfect. I knew they never would be. But I felt sure that God's grace would be sufficient for all the days ahead of us.

As I sit here now, I remember my wedding day. It was a glorious time for me. That first ring, which (by the way) I still have, was received with great joy. The glory and joy that accompanied that first ring, however, pales when compared with the joyful and glorious receiving of that second ring. Something of great value in my personal life was replaced with something that, for many reasons, turned out to be even better than the original.

In 2 Corinthians 3:7–4:6, Paul explains how the Old Covenant, which was of great value, had to be replaced with the New Covenant—one that is, for precise reasons, much better than the first. Even though the Old Covenant displayed God's glory, it paled in comparison with the coming of Christ and the New Covenant. The "fullness" of God's glory is seen in

Christ and His redemptive work, making the New Covenant far outshine the Old.

In this passage, Paul uses the imagery of a veil to compare and contrast the Old and New Covenants. As he paints a word picture of veiled and unveiled faces, hearts, and minds, he reveals three specific ways that the New Covenant is superior to the Old. The superiority of the New Covenant rests in the fact that: it leads to *life rather than death*, it results in *righteousness rather than condemnation*, and it is *permanent rather than temporary*. As I guide you through this study of 2 Corinthians 3:7–4:6 I want to help you understand the superiority of the New Covenant. I also want you to realize that the New Covenant not only reflects superior characteristics, the New Covenant is best reflected through superior character.

In chapter 2, "Letters Written on Human Hearts," we studied in detail the first superior characteristic of the New Covenant: it leads to life instead of death. Second Corinthians 4:3-4 further explains this issue of *life* and *death* by describing Satan's role. As the "god of this world," Satan is the unseen power behind all unbelief and ungodliness. He "veils" or blinds the minds of unbelievers so that they do not accept the truth of the Gospel message—even when it is clearly presented. Anyone who seeks salvation and eternal life through any means other than Jesus Christ will perish. Those who are perishing are those who habitually allow Satan to blind them through their choices and decisions.

A friend of mine gave me a large box of assorted chocolates for my birthday. I had been dieting (as usual) but this time I had been doing well. I didn't want to pull my usual trick and eat the whole box, so I told myself sternly that I would eat only one. What pressure! I knew I had to pick just the right one. It needed to be one that would satisfy me—preferably a caramel or a coconut. I was tempted to punch little holes in the bottom of each piece of candy to insure a right choice but I knew that would get me in big trouble with the rest of my family, so I began to think things through. Should I pick the big square one? Caramels are usually square—but then so are those awful fruit nuggets! Perhaps I would have a better chance of finding a coconut because they're usually round and there were more round ones in the box than square ones. My conversation with myself went on for quite some time, but even so, when I finally made my choice, I had no guarantee of satisfaction.

Life is like choosing from a large box of assorted "choices." Satan tempts us to pick and choose by our own perspective and fleshly desires, relying on visible, temporal criteria. When we yield and make choices and decisions by these standards, Satan succeeds in narrowing our vision. We gorge ourselves on things of this world which separate us from God and lead to our death. But these choices, though they taste good at the time, never satisfy.

We can choose, however, to turn to Christ to free us from sin. Second Corinthians 3:16 promises us that when we do, our veil of blindness is removed, and we can make choices from a perspective that leads to eternal life.

The Bible closely links the heart and mind (Mark 7:20-23); when Christ removes the veil of the mind, the heart is also unveiled. The heart that once was hardened to spiritual things becomes soft and moldable. That person becomes a new creation through the indwelling of the Holy Spirit. Old things pass away, and all things become new (2 Corinthians 5:17). The new believer can now partake of the second superior characteristic of the New Covenant—*righteousness* rather than *condemnation*. This righteousness is both objective (justification) and personal (sanctification).

"Justification" is a "privilege" that accompanies one's conversion. It means that a person is made pure and is put in right standing with God through the blood of Jesus (Isaiah 1:18). Sins are not only forgiven, they are forgotten (Hebrews 10:17). "Sanctification" is the "process" that results in holiness. It takes place as a person strives to become Christlike, by choosing to obey God's Word and surrendering to His will. The power of the Holy Spirit not only liberates the believer to follow God's commandments, it also initiates a desire to do so. Freed from the bondage of the law, sin, and death and motivated by love for God rather than fear, the believer is able to partake of the Lord's glory and reflect it to others.

Just as an ugly little worm can hide itself in a cocoon and gradually, over a period of time, emerge as a beautiful butterfly, we in our ugly sinful state can hide ourselves in God's grace, and gradually be transformed into His likeness with ever-increasing glory!

This ever-increasing glory marks those who have experienced God's mercy and are ministers of the New Covenant. It is symbolic of the *permanent* and effective character of the New Covenant, while the fading glory that shone on Moses' face symbolizes the *temporary* and inadequate character of the Old Covenant. Jesus, the perfect sacrifice, offered in complete submission, replaces all previous sacrifices. While the work of the levitical priests was never done, Christ's work as the High Priest is complete. His sacrifice atoned for all sins for all time.

On a more personal level, I challenge you to consider the "permanence" of your commitment to Christ. How effectively and consistently do you reflect His glory? What are you doing to develop the superior character that Paul says (2 Corinthians 4:1-3) a minister of the New

Covenant should have? As a child of God you have not only been called to an eternal hope, but you have been called to communicate God's grace to others who need that hope. "Be diligent to present yourself approved to God as a workman who does not need to be ashamed, handling accurately the word of truth" (2 Timothy 2:15, NASB).

In order to be a reflector of God's glory and truth, you must "reflect" upon God's Word *daily*. You must *personally* enter the holy of holies to *privately* fellowship with Him, so that you can *permanently* capture His reflection in a life-changing way. Too often Christians skip the private times of worship, believing that they need only to "tap" into God's glory through others, such as pastors, retreat speakers, etc. This "second-hand" glory is great for awhile, but it fades quickly. Only to the extent that you personally behold God and His Word will you be able to reflect Him to others! As a minister of the New Covenant, displaying an unveiled face, heart, and mind, you are to continually "Behold and Surrender," so that those around you who are still veiled may have the opportunity to "Behold and Believe!"

❦ GETTING INVOLVED ❦

As you continue keeping your *Life Action Diary*, rejoice and take courage in the benefits and privileges that are yours through the New Covenant!

SUNDAY: Read Romans 3:9-30.
Application:

Action:

MONDAY: Read Romans 8:9-17.
Application:

Action:

TUESDAY: Read Hebrews 2:9-18.
Application:

Action:

WEDNESDAY: Read Hebrews 4:1-16.
Application:

Action:

THURSDAY: Read Hebrews 6:9-20.
Application:

Action:

FRIDAY: Read Hebrews 7:22-28.
Application:

Action:

SATURDAY: Read Hebrews 10:19-25.
Application:

Action:

❧ GROWING INTIMATE ❧

Partners in Prayer

Pen and Paper Prayer

CHAPTER FOUR

TREASURE IN

❧ GATHERING INFORMATION ❧

1. What are your greatest treasures? Have the treasures of your life changed over the years? Explain.

Read 2 Corinthians 4:7-18.
2. What is the "treasure" referred to in verse 7? (If you are not sure, review 2 Corinthians 4:4-6 and read 1 Thessalonians 2:4.)

What do you think "jars of clay" (NIV) or "earthen vessels" (KJV), (NASB) represent in verse 7? (Refer to Isaiah 64:8.)

Name at least two adjectives that describe the weaknesses of a piece of pottery. How can you relate these concepts to your life as God's clay vessel?

What does Paul say is the purpose of keeping the "treasure" of the Gospel in "jars of clay"?

How do your weaknesses help fulfill this purpose? (See 2 Corinthians 12:9-10.)

3. In verses 8-9 Paul describes four ways in which he was a *victim* and yet a *victor* over adversity. Write the words and phrases on the chart on page 37 that Paul uses to explain how he is a victim and the corresponding way that he is a victor.

Victim   **Victor**

Have you, like Paul, ever been a victim for the sake of the Gospel? Are you under this kind of attack now? How can you know Christ's victory in this circumstance?

4. Read and summarize the following Scriptures:

Romans 8:16-18

Romans 8:35-37

Galatians 2:20

In light of these Scriptures, explain what it means to carry both the death and life of Jesus in our bodies.

5. Look again at 2 Corinthians 4:8-12. In what ways were the apostles "given over to death" for the sake of Jesus?

Read 2 Corinthians 11:21-30. How did Paul suffer for the sake of Jesus?

What was Paul's attitude toward suffering—what purpose did he see in it?

Meditate on 2 Corinthians 4:10-12. What sufferings do you carry?

Are you allowing God to use your sufferings to bring "life" to others? How?

6. According to 2 Corinthians 4:13-14, what should our faith cause us to do? What is our message to be?

What could you do personally to become a better spokeswoman for Christ?

7. Look again at 2 Corinthians 4:13-18. In the midst of his sufferings, Paul was comforted in knowing that one day he would be raised from the dead to live with Christ. Read the following passages and make notes.

Ephesians 1:13-14

1 Corinthians 15:20-25

1 Thessalonians 4:13-18

According to these passages, how can you be assured of your resurrection?

When and how will your resurrection take place?

8. Second Corinthians 4:16 begins with the word "therefore" and then speaks of the renewal of our inner beings. How can the hope of your own personal resurrection *renew* you when you suffer?

9. Considering how Paul suffered as recorded in 2 Corinthians 11:21-33, why do you think that he could speak in 2 Corinthians 4:17 of suffering as "light and momentary troubles"?

How can the following Scriptures help you adopt Paul's perspective?

Philippians 3:20-21

Colossians 3:1-4

Romans 12:1-2

10. Read 1 Peter 1:6-8 and James 1:3-4, 12. According to these verses, why ought you to try to maintain your faith even during a time of hardship? What, in these verses, encourages you to make that effort?

11. This week, how will you set your heart and mind on eternal things, so that you can remain steadfast in your faith?

For Extra Challenge
What can the passages below add to your understanding of Paul's word picture of clay jars in 2 Corinthians 4?

Psalm 90:4
Psalm 107:1-2
Romans 6:5
Romans 8:17
Romans 8:24
1 Corinthians 9:16
Ephesians 3:14-19
Philippians 3:8-10
Colossians 3:10-17
Hebrews 11:1-2, 6

❦ *GAINING INSIGHT* ❦

In old farm days, families stored their vital food supply in clay crocks. These containers were not made of precious metal or embellished with fine decorations. They were frail vessels of clayware. But without them the life of the home could not continue.[1]

As Christians, we common vessels of clay hold within us a treasure that also gives life—abundant and eternal life. Our treasure, God's message of salvation, nourishes us with the "bread of life" (John 6:35). The word picture "treasure in jars of clay" is the way Paul paints the Gospel in 2 Corinthians 4:7-18. Paul emphasizes that because of the weak and fragile state of our human container, God is able to clearly display His own enormous power and the power of His Gospel treasure. We, as His Gospel treasurers, need only concentrate on maintaining the correct perspective. Let's take a look at what this passage reveals about this *power* and *perspective*.

The Gospel treasure exhibits God's power in five specific ways. It *restores, redeems, resurrects, renews,* and *rewards* the one who possesses it. First, if we look at 2 Corinthians 4:8-12, we recognize that God's power working within *restores* not only us but others also. It restores us by giving strength and hope in the midst of our suffering. The Christian life does not exempt one from adversity. We, like Paul in verses 8 and 9, will inevitably be faced with adversity, but we can also be faithful by relying upon God's power and not on our own. We can become more than conquerors through Christ, and as others witness our obedient life, they too can be spiritually restored. We can find joy in the midst of our sufferings knowing that as we share in the sufferings of Christ (Philippians 3:10), our reflections of Him may lead someone else to eternal life.

Never have I realized this more than with my friend, Liz Matz, whom I met two years ago. Liz suffers from rheumatoid arthritis—as I have since 1976. The orthopedic doctor, who corrected my own deformity and relieved intense pain in my left foot, asked me to discuss the excellent results of my surgery with Liz. He hoped I could encourage her to undergo the same procedure.

My first meeting with Liz lasted four hours! I could not tell her about the success of my surgery without explaining God's faithfulness. Our common suffering gave me the opportunity to share the Gospel which she absorbed like a sponge. Liz had always been a religious person, but she had missed the message of a personal relationship with Christ. For months, she had felt discouraged and depressed, trying to endure her pain while fulfilling the roles of wife and mother of two young children. Liz was amazed at my response to an adversity she knew well. My deteriorating "jar of clay" reflected God's power—not human effort. As a result, Liz is experiencing today (for herself) God's all-surpassing power through the Gospel treasure, which she holds within her heart. The suffering that is at work within me allowed eternal life to be at work within Liz! This is 2 Corinthians 4:12 in action.

Second, the power of the Gospel treasure *redeems* us. Biblically, to "redeem" means to pay a penalty or a ransom in order to set someone free from something bad. As Christians, we have been redeemed from the power of sin and death by the precious blood of Jesus Christ. On the cross, Jesus bore the penalty for our sins. Psalm 107:2 states, "Let the redeemed of the Lord say so"(NASB). Those of us who have accepted Christ's sacrifice through faith and have been made into new creations are to tell the news to others. Our faith, according to verse 13, should cause us to testify to the work of Christ, so that more and more people can know Him. I remember when my children were young how they would run to me and excitedly tell me about the treasure they had found in their box of Cracker Jacks. Well, as Christians, we have found the ultimate of all treasures: Jesus Christ! We must run and excitedly tell others what He has accomplished on the cross and what He is doing in our lives.

Third, God's all-surpassing power *resurrects*. Christ's resurrection guarantees the resurrection of believers (1 Thessalonians 4:13-18). In this fact we find a hope and comfort that is foreign to nonbelievers. We have nothing to fear—not even death itself—because we have at our disposal a resurrection power sufficient for any trial of life—and one that is greater than death. Our faith is strengthened and our courage increased by the knowledge that God will one day wipe away our tears, as we enter His presence to live with Him eternally in a place where there is no mourning, crying, or pain (Revelation 21:4). This fact can transform how we view earthly suffering.

Fourth, the power of God working within us *renews*. Although outwardly we are wasting away we do not have to lose heart, because inwardly we are being renewed day-by-day (2 Corinthians 4:16). As a woman in my forties I greatly rejoice in this scriptural encouragement! In the past few years, my body has developed every sign I've ever seen of middle-age. There was a time when experiencing the negative aspects of the aging process would have caused me great distress. But now I am thankful that I can peacefully accept the fact that even though my physical beauty cannot increase, my inner beauty can. My beauty can be the kind that doesn't fade—that of a gentle and quiet spirit (1 Peter 3:4)—if I allow the indwelling Christ to daily renew my inner nature by rooting and grounding me in His love.

The outward wasting away Paul refers to is more serious than experiencing the deteriorations of middle age. Paul's physical, mental, and emotional sufferings for Christ's sake had taken their toll, but he was able to press on because spiritually he grew stronger—even as physically he grew weaker.

Are things such as fatigue, pain, or criticism causing you to lose your spiritual resilience? Let Paul's example challenge you to renew your commitment to serve Christ. Though your flesh fails, God is the strength of your heart (Psalm 73:26). Don't let today's adversity keep you from tomorrow's *reward*. In fact, you might consider viewing your adversity as an advantage. According to Paul, your troubles are privileges, because they are achieving for you an eternal weight of glory. We are not sure what form this glorious reward will take, but we know that the thought of it caused Paul to refer to his horrendous afflictions as 'light and momentary." How can we adopt his "perspective"?

Paul instructs us to "fix our eyes" on that which is unseen and eternal. We cannot see Christ or the hope that is ours because of the Gospel treasure in us, but these realities, when viewed through the "lens" of faith, provide us with an eternal perspective. Focusing on things from this perspective shatters the "magnifying glass" of fear and diminishes the intensity of the difficulties of life.

What in your life is causing you to experience "blurred vision"? Have you lost sight of the visible way God desires to reflect His power and Gospel through you—a simple vessel of clay? As a treasurer of His Gospel, it is important that you continually examine the condition of your jar of clay. Are you usable? Do you allow Him to restore you so that He can restore others through you? Do you tell others about your redemption so that they can be redeemed? Does your life reflect His resurrection power and does your attitude reflect the hope of that resurrection? Are you willing to suffer in order to receive an as yet undefined reward from God? Remember to continually focus your vision on Christ, so that you maintain a right perspective. Oh, and don't forget: Never try to hide your weaknesses. They are "visual aids" through which God's glory and power can shine to the world!

❧ *GETTING INVOLVED* ❧

Continue writing in your *Life Action Diary*. Allow these passages to encourage you as you display the Gospel to others through your sufferings, weaknesses, and words.

SUNDAY: Read 2 Timothy 2:20-26.
Application:

Action:

MONDAY: Read John 15:1-8.
Application:

Action

TUESDAY: Read Matthew 16:24-27.
Application:

Action:

WEDNESDAY: Read 1 Peter 4:12-19.
Application:

Action:

THURSDAY: Read Colossians 4:2-6.
Application:

Action:

FRIDAY: Read Romans 8:31-39.
Application:

Action:

SATURDAY: Read 1 Peter 5:6-11.
Application:

Action:

❧ *GROWING INTIMATE* ❧

Partners in Prayer

Pen and Paper Prayer

CHAPTER FIVE

DWELLING IN

Earthly Tents

⚜ *GATHERING INFORMATION* ⚜

1. How would you describe the type of dwelling a tent provides? How can you relate these adjectives to your human body?

Read 2 Corinthians 5:1-10.
 2. What words and phrases here create a sense of longing?

What does Paul mean by "earthly tent" (NIV, NASB) or "earthly house" (KJV) in verse 1?

Read Acts 18:1-3 to find out why this word picture was meaningful to Paul.

3. Paul says in 2 Corinthians 5:1 that God is building an eternal body for us in heaven. Read 1 Corinthians 15:35-44. In what ways can you expect your resurrected heavenly body to be different from your earthly body?

Read 1 Corinthians 15:51-52 and 1 Thessalonians 4:13-18. Under what circumstances will you receive this heavenly body?

How long will it take for you to be "clothed" in your new body?

Paul ends his 1 Thessalonians passage with the statement that we are to *encourage* one another with these words. How can the promise of a resurrected body encourage you today?

4. Look more carefully at 2 Corinthians 5:2-4. What words does Paul use to describe a person who has not yet received a heavenly body?

What caused Paul to "groan"? (See also Romans 8:18-25.)

In what ways can you relate to these groanings?

Focus on 2 Corinthians 5:5-8. Paul speaks of "guarantees" and "confidence." Why?

What was Paul's response to the fact that while he was on earth he was "away from the Lord?"

How does his response compare with your own feelings about life and death?

5. Read Revelation 4:1-11 and 21:1-5. What will it be like to be "at home with the Lord"?

Read Revelation 21:10–22:5 and take a moment to imagine your home to come. What do you *long for* in your heavenly home?

6. What "purpose" does Paul speak of in 2 Corinthians 5:5?

What does the Holy Spirit guarantee believers? (See also Ephesians 1:13-14.)

Look up the words "deposit" and "guarantee" (NIV), "pledge"

(NASB), and "earnest" (KJV) in a dictionary. Explain the significance of these words as used in 2 Corinthians 5:5.

7. Paul says in 2 Corinthians 5:8 that it is his goal to please the Lord. Study the passages below to find out what attitudes, thoughts, and actions please God.

Hebrews 11:6

Colossians 1:10-12

1 Thessalonians 4:1-12

In view of these passages, what are some areas of your life that need to become more pleasing to God? How can you begin to make changes?

Why might 2 Corinthians 5:10 encourage you to please God?

8. What are some ways in which 2 Corinthians 5:1-10 gives hope and comfort concerning death? Give some examples from your own life.

9. Have you ever been afraid to die? Are you afraid now?

How can this passage comfort you?

With whom could you share this hope and comfort? Ask the Lord for opportunities.

10. Practice sharing the good news of Christ with a Christian friend. You may want to use a tool such as the "Four Spiritual Laws" to help get you started. Keep in mind that the truth of this lesson can only

comfort someone if he or she already knows Christ and is bound for heaven.

For Extra Challenge
Second Corinthians 5:10 refers to the "judgment seat of Christ." How do the following Scriptures help you to understand this judgment in relation to Christians?

Matthew 16:27
Romans 14:10-18
Ephesians 2:8-10
Ephesians 5:1-21
Ephesians 6:7-8
Revelation 22:12-17

What do the passages above add to your understanding of Paul's word picture of tents in 2 Corinthians 5:1-10?

❦ GAINING INSIGHT ❦

Are you afraid to die? Do you know anyone who fears death? Perhaps you know someone who is dying or, because of a terminal illness, will soon face death. Paul's words in 2 Corinthians 5:1-10 can bring you comfort and meaning because he teaches there about that unknown segment of our Christian experience called "death." I realize that this last statement is a paradox. But, for the Christian, death is not a period at the end of the sentence of life. It is a colon announcing that something is coming after this life.

Paul wants us to know that what death ushers in for the Christian is far better than what we had on earth. So the purpose of Paul's word pictures in these verses is to build confidence in the Christian regarding death. Paul explains that we can courageously face suffering and death because we have the blessed assurance of three things: the *possession* of a glorified body, the *pledge* of the Holy Spirit, and the *presence* of Christ. As you personally experience this assurance, I challenge you to use the truths of these verses to comfort others.

In verse 1, Paul states that we can know we will one day *possess new glorified bodies*. He is emphatic. It is a fact that is not to be questioned. If you have any doubts, allow God's Word to erase them. Philippians 3:20-21 promises us that our bodies will be transformed, and 1 Corinthians 15:35-54 gives us details of this transformation. Remember, all Scripture is inspired by God (2 Timothy 3:16), and it is impossible for God to lie (Hebrews 6:18). God wants the reality of a new body to be a source of divine comfort for you when you face suffering and death.

The first word picture Paul paints illustrates the differences between our earthly bodies and our future heavenly bodies. He likens our earthly bodies to tents, temporary dwellings that are easily dismantled and destroyed. But our heavenly bodies are described as houses built by God, perfect and eternal.

Paul's second word picture portrays our spiritual bodies as something we put on like a garment. Won't it be wonderful to one day hang up our tattered earthly garb and slip into something more eternal? For those of us who suffer physically, won't the lack of pain feel glorious? For those of us who have worn obvious imperfections, we can expect a "perfect" fit this time. We are children of the King, and when we go to live with Him, we will be adorned in splendor.

As a mother it has always given me great pleasure to buy clothes for my children—especially when they were in the infant to 6x sizes. I could transform my son Shawn into a sailor, a baseball player, or a miniature jogger. As for my daughter Shannon, I kept her covered with lace, ruffles, and bows from head to toe—the more the better. If we, as earthly parents, delight in providing temporal, unimportant clothing for our children, can you imagine the joy our Heavenly Father must feel when He transforms us with eternal clothing of the utmost significance?

Our second point of assurance when facing suffering and death comes from the *pledge of the Holy Spirit.* "In Him, you also, after listening to the message of truth, the Gospel of your salvation—having also believed, you were sealed in Him with the Holy Spirit of promise, who is given as a pledge of our inheritance, with a view to the redemption of God's *own* possession, to the praise of His glory" (Ephesians 1:13-14, NASB). The Holy Spirit is our "guarantee" that we will be raised up and clothed in a resurrection body! We are "marked" as belonging to Christ; His presence within us "seals" us until the day God chooses to "redeem" us, His purchases.

The last time our family went to Kings Island, a large amusement park in Ohio, we purchased our tickets as usual at the main gate. These tickets not only gave us entry to the park but also gave us access to every ride available. Shortly after we were inside, I realized I had left my arthritis medication in the car. Before I returned to the car, the official stamped my hand with ink that was invisible to the natural eye. But when I approached the gate to reenter, the official placed my hand under an ultraviolet light, which clearly revealed the day's date. The mark on my hand guaranteed my entrance into the park so that I could take advantage of privileges purchased for me earlier.

The Holy Spirit is the identifying mark of every true believer. Even though He cannot be seen with the natural eye, He guarantees our entry into the gates of heaven. There we will be able to take full advantage of the blessings that Christ purchased for us on the cross long ago—including that of a glorified body.

Last, we can face suffering and death with confidence because of the assurance we receive from the *presence of Christ* with us. As a result of our faith, we experience the "unseen" presence of Christ. As we abide in

Him and He in us we are able to do all things through Christ who strengthens us. When we die, we will experience a more profound form of intimate fellowship with Christ. We will be in His presence and see Him face to face. Christ's presence not only gives us confidence to live but also confidence to die.

Like Paul, we can take courage in the fact that when we die we go immediately to be with the Lord (2 Corinthians 5:8). Upon death, I believe that we leave our earthly bodies in a disembodied or "unclothed" state, as Paul describes it, and we go to wait with the Lord until all spiritual bodies are distributed at the trumpet's sound.

What then is our responsibility until we go to be with the Lord? Whether here on earth and physically away from the Lord, or at home in heaven and dwelling in His presence, we must make it our goal to please Him. As His daughter, you want to please Him as an expression of your love and devotion.

Paul, however, gives us another reason to please God. He reminds us that, as Christians, God will judge us for the deeds we have done while living in our earthly tents. We will each be held accountable for our lives and service. This accountability does not yield righteousness but rather rewards. Our salvation is not a result of our works, which comes by faith alone. Our works, however, are a result of our salvation. It is our works that will be evaluated and judged.

God's Word is full of advice on how to please the Lord, and we must obediently follow it. As we do, God will use us to draw others to Him. We need to make the most of every opportunity He gives us to share the "Good News" of the Gospel of Jesus Christ. It is our responsibility to introduce others to the source of confident living and dying so that they, like us, can know the peace and joy of one day having eternal houses in heaven.

Think of the last time you bought something new to wear. Didn't you look forward to showing it to someone close to you? Now, envision yourself, being clothed by the Master Tailor in your eternal house. Full of excitement, you turn around, anxious to show your new dwelling to a member of your immediate family—or maybe a close relative, or special friend, perhaps even a fellow-employee. . . . Are they there?

Ask God today what you can do to show them the way.

❦ *GETTING INVOLVED* ❦

Continue journaling in your *Life Action Diary*. The following Scripture meditations will help you face suffering with God's strength and perspective.

SUNDAY: Read 1 John 5:3-5, 11-13.
Application:

Action:

MONDAY: Read Philippians 3:7-21.
Application:

Action:

TUESDAY: Read Ephesians 2:1-7.
Application:

Action:

WEDNESDAY: Read Philippians 1:21-30.
Application:

Action:

THURSDAY: Read Romans 8:26-39.
Application:

Action:

FRIDAY: Matthew 6:1-6.
Application:

Action:

SATURDAY: Read 2 Peter 1:2-15.
Application:

Action

❦ *GROWING INTIMATE* ❦

Partners in Prayer

Pen and Paper Prayer

CHAPTER SIX

UNEQUALLY

❦ *GATHERING INFORMATION* ❦

1. Have you ever seen or participated in a three-legged race? What kind of person makes the best partner for you? Why?

   Read Deuteronomy 22:10. What did God's Old Testament Law prohibit? What are some possible reasons why God gave this restriction?

Read 2 Corinthians 6:14–7:1.

2. How might God's command against unequal yoking of animals relate to Paul's concerns in this word picture?

3. Consider Paul's rhetorical questions in 1 Corinthians 6:14-16. (Note: Belial is another name for Satan) From these five sets of relationships, what are some reasons why a believer should not enter a partnership or binding relationship with an unbeliever?

4. Is Paul saying that Christians should have nothing to do with unbelievers? Explain.

   How does 1 Corinthians 5:9-10 help qualify this command?

5. In 2 Corinthians 6:16, Paul speaks of God's people as "the temple of God." Read his further comments on that subject in 1 Corinthians 3:16-17 and 6:15-20. According to these texts, what makes you a "temple" of the living God?

What responsibilities do you have as His temple?

Where do you, as God's temple, need repairs or renovations? How will you begin to address these areas?

6. What four things does God promise those in whom He dwells? (2 Corinthians 6:16)

In Leviticus 26:12, God used this same language when He established His covenant with Israel. Now Paul tells us that God extends these promises to any who have faith in Christ. What do each of these promises of 2 Corinthians 6:16 mean to you?

7. In verse 17, who are we told to be separate from and why? What are some specific ways that we can separate ourselves without segregating ourselves from the world?

8. Read 1 John 2:15-17 and Ephesians 5:1-10. How does the information in these passages relate to the idea of separation?

In view of these texts, give some examples of "unclean things" that Christians should avoid. What makes them unclean?

9. Reread 2 Corinthians 6:18. What is God's promise to you here?

According to John 1:12-13 and John 3:3-7, how do you become God's daughter?

If you are not sure that you have been adopted into the family of God, pause and pray a prayer of faith in which you ask forgiveness of your sins, and invite Christ into your life as your Savior. Write your prayer here.

10. Put into your own words the command given in 2 Corinthians 7:1.

Give examples of practices that contaminate our bodies. Our spirits.

How do these things work against the work of the Holy Spirit?

11. Read Romans 12:1-2. What information here inspires you to live in a holy way?

12. Read Jude 24-25. How can this verse encourage you as you strive to be holy?

When Jude says that God is "able to keep you from falling," does that mean you will never fall? How would you describe your part in keeping yourself holy?

13. In view of your study of this word picture, which of your own "yokes" ought you to be examining? Talk to God about it.

For Extra Challenge
What can the passages below add to your understanding of the predicament of being unequally yoked?

1 Corinthians 7:12-16
1 Corinthians 10:1-10, 27-33
Ephesians 4:30
1 Thessalonians 5:19
1 Peter 3:1-2
2 Peter 1:2-4

❦ *GAINING INSIGHT* ❦

At first we might think it strange that God included in His laws to Israel the words, "Do not plow with an ox and a donkey yoked together." The reason behind this law, however, shows that it is more than just an arbitrary restriction. God's laws, both in the Old Testament and the New, were intended to protect His people. Due to the difference in strength and size, an ox and a donkey cannot pull a plow evenly, and the unequal pull causes the weaker animal to suffer.

God had this issue of suffering in mind when He inspired Paul to write to the believers in Corinth, "Do not be yoked together with unbelievers" (2 Corinthians 6:14). Paul's word picture here is meant to warn Christians that if a believer and an unbeliever bind themselves together to plow the fields of life, the unequal pull between them will surely cause suffering.

In 2 Corinthians 6:14–7:1, Paul gives us three principles to guide us: *be selective, be separate,* and *be sanctified.* His instruction is meant to protect us from compromising God's standards or jeopardizing our Christian witness.

In Paul's first letter to the Corinthians, he warned them to flee from idolatry (1 Corinthians 10:14). Some Corinthians, however, continued to participate in pagan practices, and Paul feared this would lead them to enter compromising alliances with unbelievers. Paul therefore advises them to *be selective* in all binding relationships. Since the unbeliever would not share the believer's values or goals, Paul questions how much compatibility can exist between the two.

As I counsel with women at retreats and seminars, one of the greatest heartaches they share is the suffering experienced by a believer married to an unbeliever. Even though each woman loves her husband, there is a void in the relationship. Although they may be compatible in many ways—sexually, intellectually—nothing can make up for the lack of spiritual compatibility. It is painful for these women to cherish a treasure (the Gospel) in which their husbands see no value.

Most of these women became Christians after they married. Some were Christians when they married but were not aware of the advice given in God's Word. Others were aware of God's Word but chose not to heed its counsel.

Perhaps you too are suffering, along with these women, because you are married to an unbeliever. What should you do? You are encouraged in 1 Corinthians 7:12-16 to stay in the relationship as long as your husband is willing and remains faithful to his marriage vows. Paul offers the hope that your continued presence will persuade your husband to follow Christ. Because of the uniqueness of the relationship, your actions speak louder than your words (1 Peter 3:1). Make sure that prayer is one of your consistent actions.

Paul also gives us the command to be *separate* from the world. We must be "in" the world, not "of" it. While we need to associate with unbelievers in order to share the Gospel with them, we must not participate in their sinful practices. This separation of our actions and attitudes must not isolate us from those who do not know Christ: "I have become all things to all men so that by all possible means I might save some," said the Apostle Paul in 1 Corinthians 9:22. If we reach out to unbelievers with love and understanding instead of condemnation, they may see something different, and yet desirable, in us.

Oil and vinegar can be mixed for a short time to serve as a flavorful salad dressing. Each component, however, always maintains its own identity. As soon as the bottle is set aside, the oil quickly separates itself from the vinegar by rising to the top. We Christians need to mix ourselves with the world to serve as a flavorful enticement for the Gospel message. But when tempted by the sins of the world we must separate ourselves so that we can rise to the top in victory.

Last, Paul commands us to be *sanctified.* "For God did not call us to be impure, but to live a holy life" (1 Thessalonians 4:7). How holy? Well, God challenges us with these words: "But just as He who called you is holy, so be holy in all you do" (1 Peter 1:15). God is our standard for holiness. We already discussed sanctification as being a process (chapter 3). We are to continually perfect our holiness. According to Webster, something is perfect if it "lacks nothing essential to the whole." It is "complete in its nature" and is of "highest excellence." As we submit ourselves in obedience, we will find ourselves being transformed into the likeness of Christ.

Second Corinthians 7:1 makes it clear that we play a significant part in our own purification. We must make choices that will consecrate and not contaminate our bodies and spirits. The power of the Holy Spirit can enable us to make those choices and abandon all compromise when we are pulled between good and evil.

While the Holy Spirit sanctifies us, the fear of the Lord ought to motivate us. Are you filled with awe, respect, and love for God because He has made you a joint heir with Jesus Christ and has given you the privilege of being His dwelling place? "Do you not know that you are a temple of God, and that the Spirit of God dwells in you?" (1 Corinthians 3:16) Your reverence for God should result in a desire for purity. And as you strengthen your temple by being *selective, separate, and sanctified,* you strengthen the church of Christ as a whole. Paul wrote in Ephesians 2:22, "In Him [Christ] you too are being built together to become a dwelling in which God lives by His Spirit."

❦ *GETTING INVOLVED* ❦

Continue journaling in your *Life Action Diary*. Use the following Scriptures to meditate on the issues of Christian distinctiveness.

SUNDAY: Read 1 Peter 1:14-23.
Application:

Action:

MONDAY: Read 1 John 1:5-10.
Application:

Action:

TUESDAY: Read 1 John 3:1-10.
Application:

Action:

WEDNESDAY: Read Matthew 6:19-24.
Application:

Action:

THURSDAY: Read Ephesians 5:1-17.
Application:

Action:

FRIDAY: Read Romans 8:5-16.
Application:

Action:

SATURDAY: Read 1 Thessalonians 4:1-8.
Application:

Action:

❦ *GROWING INTIMATE* ❦

Partners in Prayer

Pen and Paper Prayer

CHAPTER SEVEN

SOWING AND

❦ *GATHERING INFORMATION* ❦

1. When have you *received* an object or a service that you greatly valued?

What have you *given* that seems to have met a particular need at just the right time?

Read 2 Corinthians 9:6-15.
2. What concepts here encourage God's people to give and also to receive gifts?

3. What relationships can you see between Paul's word picture of a farmer's work and the act of giving?

When have you experienced the principle described in verse 6?

4. What is the most serious financial concern in your life today?

Note: As you work through this chapter, make 3 x 5 note cards of the Scripture references that address this obstacle. Memorize the verses that encourage you.

5. Read 2 Corinthians 9:7 and Exodus 35:4-10. According to these texts, what principles should guide our giving?

Do you follow these principles in your own life? Why or why not?

In what areas, besides financial giving, do you think these principles could apply? Explain.

6. In 2 Corinthians 9:1, Paul spoke of giving as "service to the saints." List some creative ways a woman of God can give generously to help meet the needs of other believers.

7. Read the passages below and make note of some additional principles that should guide your giving.

Matthew 6:1-4

Matthew 6:19-21

1 Corinthians 16:1-2

Deuteronomy 15:10-11

In view of these texts, what are some of the reasons that God instructs His people to give?

Select one concept from one of the texts above and write how you can better put it into practice.

8. Return to 2 Corinthians 9. According to verses 8-11, how does God reward the generous giver?

Summarize each of the following promises God makes to those who give.

Philippians 4:19

Matthew 6:3

Proverbs 11:25

Proverbs 19:17

Give one or two examples of how you have seen these promises realized in your life.

9. Read again 2 Corinthians 9:12-15. What reasons (other than personal reward) does Paul cite here for generous giving?

What effects does generous giving have on relationships among God's people?

10. Read 2 Corinthians 8:9 and Philippians 4:19. How is the idea of wealth, as it is presented in these texts, different than the normal worldview?

11. God sets an example to His people with His own giving. Paul speaks, in 2 Corinthians 9:15 of God's "indescribable" (NIV, NASB) or "unspeakable" (KJV) gift. What is this gift? (See also John 3:16-18 and Romans 6:23.)

How would you describe the *indescribable* gift?

How does God's gift illustrate the principles of giving taught in 2 Corinthians 9:7?

In what ways does God's gift challenge you to give?

12. What do you learn from the following examples of giving?

Mark 12:41-44

2 Corinthians 8:1-5

Does a person need to be wealthy in order to give to others? Explain.

13. How can riches actually make giving more difficult? (See Matthew 19:21-26 and 1 Timothy 6:17-19.)

14. Many biblical passages speak of a "tithe." Read the passages below and answer these questions: What is a tithe? How does tithing relate to generous giving? Does the principle of tithing apply only to money?

Genesis 14:17-20

Malachi 3:8-10

Matthew 23:23

15. Read Philippians 4:14-19 and Hebrews 13:16. How does God view the gifts we give?

16. Take mental stock of your own habits and motives for giving. In view of your study in this chapter, what do you feel that you are doing right and ought to continue?

What changes in your giving patterns would you like to make?

❦ *GAINING INSIGHT* ❦

"But the bag said 'fertilizer,' " I wailed in my defense.

My husband looked at me in disbelief. It was inconceivable to him that any mature adult could mistake grass seed for fertilizer!

At the time we were in our early twenties, and had just moved into our first house. We were working diligently to beautify our yard. Joe had spent hours on Monday evening digging a large flower bed for me. The soil, which contained a lot of clay, was not the best. Before he left for work on Tuesday, Joe instructed me to mix a generous amount of fertilizer into the soil before planting any flowers. He said the fertilizer was in the garage.

When I went to look I found two bags marked "fertilizer." One was already open, so I decided to use it. I wasn't sure how much to use, but since Joe had said to be generous I decided the more the better. I made sure I sowed the fertilizer deeply, and that I mixed it thoroughly into the soil. Then I spent the rest of the afternoon planting my flowers. I wanted to surprise Joe by having the bed completed by the time he came home.

Not only did I surprise him, but he surprised me. He informed me that after planting grass seed in the thin patches of our yard, he had stored the extra seed in an empty fertilizer bag! Together, we dug up the flowers and tried to rectify my mistake. I'm afraid, however, we were pulling grass from that flower bed all summer long. I learned the hard way that you definitely reap what you sow!

In 2 Corinthians 9:6-15, Paul discusses this law of the harvest as being operative in the life of the Christian. He portrays Christian giving with the imagery of sowing and reaping to teach principles about giving. As Paul paints his word picture, he emphasizes *the rules* and *the results* of generous giving, and portrays Jesus—God's indescribable gift—as *the reason* for our generous giving.

In verses 6 and 7, Paul suggests some guidelines or *rules* for giving. He first exhorts the Corinthians (and us) to give generously. The image of the harvest depicts the freedom of the sower to plant as much or as little as he desires. At the same time, however, the imagery reinforces the idea that generosity pays high dividends. Paul says the same principle applies to our giving.

Although Paul encourages us to give liberally, it is clear from this passage that the spirit and attitude with which we give is more important than the gift itself. Pure motives must guide the way we give as much as the amount. Paul insists that our giving be voluntary, in accordance with what we individually determine in our hearts before God. It should not be the result of external pressure or compulsion. These guidelines help us to give cheerfully, not grudgingly, and this pleases God.

There is true joy to be found in meeting the needs of others. Even when our financial reserves are low, there is always someone who has less. Paul says, "Our desire is not that others might be relieved while you are hard pressed, but that there might be equality. At the present time your plenty will supply what they need, so that in turn their plenty will supply what you need" (2 Corinthians 8:13-14).

Our gifts, of course, do not have to be money. I encourage you to be creative in your giving. My neighbor, Elaine Hoffmann, is a great example of a creative giver. Elaine figured out how to give to the church by having a Tupperware party in her home. The Tupperware incentive plan is similar to any other kind of home party. The hostess is awarded points according to the dollars spent on Tupperware at her party, and these points are redeemable toward Tupperware products. I have had many Tupperware parties and was always excited to cash in my points for "free" Tupperware items for myself. Elaine, on the other hand, spent her points on Tupperware toys which she gave to her church nursery. Her example of giving challenges me. How about you?

In verses 8-14 we discover that generous giving reaps three positive *results*. It enriches the giver, encourages the recipient, and enhances unity in the body of Christ.

In his word picture Paul parallels God's liberality in nature with His liberality in grace, emphasizing the rewards of generous giving. Paul depicts God as the supplier who not only supplies but multiplies the resources of the generous giver, so that He is able to reap a full harvest of good deeds. God promises to meet *all* of our needs according to His riches in glory (Philippians 4:19), and in return, He expects us to meet the needs of others. He desires to make us rich (enrich us) in every way so that we can be generous on every occasion (2 Corinthians 9:11). God's riches embrace far more than the world's idea of riches. This is evident when we consider 2 Corinthians 8:9: "For you know the grace of our Lord Jesus Christ, that though He was rich, yet for your sakes He became poor, so that you through His poverty might become rich." Our goal must not be to acquire possessions but to alleviate needs.

In the past few years, a simple slogan has become popular at Christmas: "Jesus is the *reason* for the season." Jesus, God's inexpressible gift, is the reason we celebrate Christmas. Our own gift-giving is symbolic of the marvelous gift God gave to us. The same generous giving which is greatly encouraged during this holiday ought to continue all year long.

This time I am challenged by the example of a close friend, Cindy Robinette. I doubt if a day goes by that Cindy does not give of herself in some way to someone else. Cindy has chosen not to get a job so that she can stay at home with her son Matthew during his preschool years. Her decision requires that she and her husband budget their money carefully. I am sure that many times she sacrifices her own needs and desires in order to "generously" give to meet the needs of others. Her gifts, which always encourage, may take the form of a greeting card which she carefully chose to say just the right thing, a spiritual book or tape, or an item that she has spent hours making by hand. Anyone who knows Cindy has in some way been blessed by her unselfish and sensitive giving. Why does she spend so much time focusing on others? I know if you asked her she would say Jesus is the reason. Personally experiencing God's love through His indescribable gift motivates her to love others with her gifts. And what does she reap? I'm sure unimaginable rewards await her in heaven, but I also know that God's all-surpassing faithfulness, unspeakable joy, and incredible love belong to her right now.

Christian, Christian, how does your garden of giving grow? Remember, everything depends on how you sow. I am sure God will be pleased with your harvest if you follow Paul's *rules,* allow yourself to be encouraged by the *results,* and focus upon Jesus as the *reason* for your sowing in the first place.

❦ *GETTING INVOLVED* ❦

Continue journaling in your *Life Action Diary*. The following Scripture passages will help you focus on the practice of giving generously.

SUNDAY: Read Proverbs 22:8-9 and 28:27.
Application:

Action:

MONDAY: Read 2 Corinthians 8:1-15.
Application:

Action:

TUESDAY: Read Psalm 112:1-9.
Application:

Action:

WEDNESDAY: Read James 2:14-18.
Application:

Action:

THURSDAY: Read Luke 18:18-30.
Application:

Action:

FRIDAY: Read Galatians 6:7-10.
Application:

Action:

SATURDAY: Read Matthew 13:1-9.
Application:

Action:

❦ GROWING INTIMATE ❦

Partners in Prayer

Pen and Paper Prayer

CHAPTER EIGHT

A THORN IN THE

❧ *GATHERING INFORMATION* ❧

1. What kinds of boasting do you hear and see around you?

When do you get annoyed by this boasting?

Do you ever wish you could boast about yourself—just a little bit? Explain.

Read 2 Corinthians 11:1-15.
2. In this passage, Paul defends his apostleship and instructs the Corinthians not to be deceived by "false apostles." In what ways does Paul express his concern for the Corinthians?

Read 2 Corinthians 11:16-30.
3. List Paul's credentials as an apostle. How do they differ from those of his opponents?

Paul says in verse 18 that he will boast. What all does he boast about?

In general, how would you describe the kinds of things Paul boasts about here?

Why do you think Paul boasts about these experiences and in this way?

What is the only real reason to boast?

Read 2 Corinthians 12:1-10.
4. What credentials does Paul add to his boast in 2 Corinthians 12:1?

Can you think of any situation today in which a woman of God might need to boast for Christ's sake? Explain.

5. Most scholars agree that Paul is speaking of himself in 2 Corinthians 12:1-6. Why do you think he uses the third person to tell of his supernatural experience, and why might he have kept it a secret for fourteen years?

Take a mental survey of some pastors and evangelists that you know, or know of. Who do you know whose motives about boasting seem similar to Paul's?

What different motives for boasting have you seen?

What impact can these observations have on your choices about whom to accept as your own leaders?

6. In verse 2, Paul talks about being taken to the "third heaven." In view of the way Paul described this event (verses 2-4), what do you think Paul heard and saw there?

Why do you think he was not permitted to tell about it?

Note: Some biblical scholars believe that Paul conceived of heaven as having three divisions: atmospheric, stellar, and spiritual (where God resided). (Read Nehemiah 9:6; 1 Kings 8:27; 2 Chronicles 2:6; and Psalm 148:4 for expressions like "heavens" and "highest heaven.") But in Paul's day there were also some who divided the heavens into five or even seven parts. It just is not clear exactly what Paul experienced and what he meant by the term "third heaven."

7. Paul also received other visions from the Lord. Read the following accounts of these visions and briefly describe the purpose for them.

Acts 16:1-10

Acts 18:1-11

Acts 22:1-15

Do you believe God gives His people visions today? Why or why not?

8. Look more carefully at 2 Corinthians 12:7-10. According to verse 7, what was the purpose of Paul's "thorn in the flesh"?

In what different ways did Paul react to his thorn?

How did Paul's thorn affect his boasting? Why?

9. Consider Paul's statement in Philippians 3:1-11. How does this passage relate to the purpose for Paul's thorn?

10. Summarize the accounts of the following two prideful men and their destinies:

2 Chronicles 26:16-21

Daniel 4:19-34

Is pride a problem in your life? How can 1 John 1:9 help you?

11. According to the following Scriptures what, besides humility, can be gained through suffering?

Romans 5:3-5

Hebrews 5:8

James 1:2-4

12. What is your "thorn in the flesh"? How do you see God using it to teach you to depend more upon His grace?

How can the following Scriptures encourage you?

Romans 8:35-39

Philippians 4:11-13

Ephesians 3:14-19

Isaiah 40:28-31

Isaiah 41:10

Begin memorizing the verses that are particularly meaningful to you.

13. Look again at 2 Corinthians 12:8. What was Paul's initial response to his "thorn"? How does Paul's response compare with that of Jesus in the garden as shown in Matthew 26:36-46?

Take stock of your response to your own "thorn." Do you continually plead with God to take away your suffering, or do you submit?

Give an example of how you might balance praying about your need with submitting to God.

14. Read Job 2:1-7. What insight does this passage give you to explain why Paul referred to his thorn as a "messenger of Satan."

Although Satan is "allowed" to attack God's servants, who sets the limits of his attacks? (Job 2:6)

15. A paradox is a statement that seems to contradict itself but expresses a truth. What paradoxes do you see in 2 Corinthians 12:9?

Explain these paradoxes in your own words.

How have you experienced one of these paradoxes in your life?

16. What was the greatest display of God's power simultaneously existing with human weakness that the world has ever known? (See Matthew 27:33-56.) Explain your answer.

17. Reread 2 Corinthians 12:9-10. Describe Paul's attitude toward his weaknesses and suffering.

In what weakness, insult, hardship, persecution, or difficulty do you need to find contentment?

How will the truths of this lesson help you trust in the grace of God more fully?

For Extra Challenge
What can the passage below add to your understanding of Paul's word picture of a thorn in the flesh as portrayed in 2 Corinthians 12:1-10?

1 Corinthians 10:13

Note: the word "temptation" in this verse can also be translated "trial." How does this promise encourage you?

Briefly review the eight lessons in this Bible study. Write one or two sentences explaining how each lesson has challenged you to know and love God more.

Chapter 1: The Fragrance of Life and Death

Chapter 2: Letters Written on Human Hearts

Chapter 3: Veiled and Unveiled Faces, Hearts, and Minds

Chapter 4: Treasure in Jars of Clay

Chapter 5: Dwelling in Earthly Tents

Chapter 6: Unequally Yoked

Chapter 7: Sowing and Reaping

Chapter 8: A Thorn in the Flesh

❦ *GAINING INSIGHT* ❦

Her screams bounced off the walls of that tiny weight room, each one piercing my heart like an arrow. As parents, we always seem to suffer "firsthand" the pain our children experience.

My daughter Shannon was only four years old at the time. Our family was vacationing in Florida, and Shannon and her brother Shawn had been playing on a teetertotter in the outdoor recreation area of our motel. Without considering how serious the consequences could be, Shawn jumped off the teetertotter without warning Shannon. Her crash to the ground left her with a large sliver of wood deeply embedded in her "derrière." As Shannon sobbed uncontrollably, hotel personnel gathered first-aid equipment, and turned the conveniently located exercise room into an emergency health care center. I stroked her hair and held her hand, as three different people, including her father, tried unsuccessfully to remove the oversized splinter. Finally, the hotel manager arrived with a topical anesthetic. By using the spray to numb the inflamed area, we were finally able to dig deep enough to remove the menacing thorn in her flesh. Needless to say, the experience remains etched in our minds.

In 2 Corinthians 12:1-10, Paul refers to an unnamed harassing affliction in his life as a "thorn in the flesh." His imagery makes it clear that this affliction, which God chose not to remove, caused him ongoing suffering and pain. Although his situation is difficult, we find that Paul, as usual, does not "complain" but instead "complies" with the will of God. Amazingly, Paul does not just "accept" and "adjust" to his weakness, he *glories* in it. As he discusses *paradise, pain,* and *perfection,* Paul uses this word picture of a thorn in the flesh to instruct the Corinthians (and us) about humility and dependence upon God.

Paul did not believe in boasting any more than in complaining, but he felt compelled. His opponents had raised questions concerning his authority as an apostle and the Corinthians had failed to speak on his behalf. "I have made a fool of myself, but you drove me to it. I ought to have been commended by you, for I am not the least inferior to the 'super-apostles,' even though I am nothing" (2 Corinthians 12:11).

In 2 Corinthians 11, Paul lists his credentials, which far outweigh those of the false apostles. Still, he adds one more qualification in chapter 12, a vision of *paradise* which God had given him fourteen years earlier. Even though Paul felt it necessary to finally divulge his experience in order to defend himself for Christ's sake, he chose not to exalt himself through elaborate details of his ecstatic experience. Paul was not interested in using his personal encounter with the Lord to gain public recognition, but was instead content with the confirmation it afforded him. For this reason, he directed all attention toward his weaknesses.

One evidence of Paul's weakness was his "thorn in the flesh." He never reveals to us what the affliction was, but he does tell us why Satan was allowed to attack him with it—to keep him humble before God. Knowing why we suffer is not a consolation most of us are given. (Job was never told the reason for his suffering.) How many times, in the midst of pain and suffering, have you cried out, "Why, Lord? Why?" without receiving an explanation? With spiritual maturity comes the realization that we do not need to know why in order to trust God. Only He knows everything and can skillfully embroider the dark threads of our life with the colorful ones, intricately creating each one of us into a special work of art which can glorify Him.

Realizing the purpose of his *pain* did not lesson the torment of the thorn for Paul. He admitted that he begged the Lord three times to remove it from his life. Think of how a child begs for something. No one can be more persistent than a child who is trying to persuade someone to give him his way. Paul petitioned the Lord intensely. His Heavenly Father, however, did not give in to his pleading. God chose to allow the suffering to remain.

God can answer our prayers in four ways. He can say "yes," "no," "wait awhile," or "I've got a better idea." In Paul's case, I think God may have been saying "I've got a better idea." God chose not to demonstrate His power in the form of healing and strength but rather in the form of grace through weakness. Through God's wondrous grace, divine power would reach *perfection* (maturity) in Paul. The awesomeness of God's promise to Paul is vividly displayed in the *Amplified Version:* "But He said to me, My grace—My favor and loving-kindness and mercy—are enough for you, [that is, sufficient against any danger and to enable you to bear the trouble manfully]; for *My* strength *and* power are made perfect—fulfilled and completed and *show themselves most effective*—in [your] weakness" (2 Corinthians 12:9a).

Just as awesome is the submission reflected in Paul's response to God's promise. Again from the *Amplified Version:* "Therefore, I will all the more gladly glory in my weaknesses *and* infirmities, that the strength *and* power of Christ, the Messiah, may rest—yes, may pitch a tent [over] and dwell—upon me" (2 Corinthians 12:9b).

Paul teaches us that a crucial aspect of submission is attitude. He does not just learn to live with his weaknesses, he learns to delight and takes pleasure in them. He finds contentment in the cross he must bear, because he knows that even though his human strength inevitably fails, the divine strength within him will prevail.

What is your attitude toward the sufferings you are facing? Adopting Paul's philosophy is not easy, but the rewards are profound. Can you imagine the differences in your life if God's power were allowed to "pitch a tent" over you. By glorying in your infirmities and weaknesses you allow this to happen.

Glorying in my weaknesses has been a hard concept for me to understand. Years of suffering finally led me to experience what Paul meant. Two major weaknesses have plagued me in my life. The first is a curvature of the spine (scoliosis) that developed when I was in fifth grade; the second is rheumatoid arthritis which struck me when I was thirty.

The curvature caused a physical deformity which made me feel inadequate in those sensitive teenage years. I doubted my own worth for many years—until I met Jesus personally. In this study I would like to share the impact 2 Corinthians 12:9 had in my life. I remember the freedom I felt when I could finally say "I accept and love myself exactly the way I am." Then I read Paul's words, and I remember thinking, "O Lord, I can accept myself, but I can never find pleasure and delight in my body the way it is." How wrong I was! The first time that a young woman accepted Christ because of my testimony, I "gloried" in my "thorn." The same is true with the rheumatoid arthritis. Liz Matz's salvation, which I shared with you in chapter 4, allows me to "glory" in this debilitating disease. Before submitting, I pleaded many more times than Paul for God to remove this painful thorn. He has not yet chosen to do so. Daily, as I battle the fatigue, pain, and deterioration of my earthly tent, I really do find that His grace allows me to bear the trouble "womanfully."

Some mechanical clocks are powered by a heavy weight. The thorns in our lives may seem like heavy weights that we must carry with us. The weight of our thorn can entangle us and thwart us completely, or we can allow it to put us in touch with the only power in our lives that can keep us going: His. Living daily with rheumatoid arthritis requires me to be constantly dependent on the Lord. I could not live victoriously without

Him. The beauty of my thorn is that this element of dependency creates a depth in my relationship with Christ that probably would not be there if I were well. And the power made available to me through His grace sufficiently energizes my service to God. On those mornings when swollen joints, stiffness, and pain tempt me to pity myself and stay in bed, my love for God and involvement with others lure me to get up and overcome!

What in your life is overpowering you? Perhaps you feel so weak from the battle that you don't think you can go on. Remember that God is strongest in the midst of your weakness. You can have a taste of paradise and perfection in the midst of your pain, by using His gift of all-sufficient grace. Begin trusting Him with the thorns in your life, and allow Him to reveal to you their tremendous value. Purpose today to allow the prism of His love to defuse the tears of your suffering into hope, promise, and power.

❦ *GETTING INVOLVED* ❦

Continue journaling in your *Life Action Diary*. The following Scripture passages focus on the purpose of our suffering.

SUNDAY: Read Hebrews 2:14-18.
Application:

Action:

MONDAY: Read 1 Peter 4:12-19.
Application

Action:

TUESDAY: Read 1 Peter 5:5-10.
Application:

Action:

WEDNESDAY: Read Jeremiah 17:5-8.
Application:

Action:

THURSDAY: Read Philippians 4:11-13 and Isaiah 58:11.
Application:

Action:

FRIDAY: Read Isaiah 55:8-11.
Application:

Action:

SATURDAY: Read 1 Corinthians 1:26-31.
Application:

Action:

❦ *GROWING INTIMATE* ❦

Partners in Prayer

Pen and Paper Prayer

❧ GUIDING INTERACTION ❧

I suggest that the first meeting be a time of fellowship and preparation for this study. Make sure that everyone in the group knows each other. Play some ice-breaker games. Pass out the books and create excitement for the topic.

Go through the *Introduction* on pages 7–9 together. Make sure everyone understands how to keep a *Life Action Diary.* Journaling, as well as making personal applications from God's Word, may be a new experience for many, so encourage them in their abilities to do this and emphasize how it can positively affect and even change their lives. Also, make sure everyone understands how and when to write their *Pen and Paper Prayer.*

If possible, record the names and addresses of all group members. In order to reach out to each member, you may want to call them or write notes of encouragement. If possible, let group members know how they can contact you.

❦ GROUP STUDY 1 ❦

Objective:
To help group members see themselves as distributors of the fragrance of Christ and to begin to fulfill this responsibility.

Leader Preparation:
1. Read and complete all parts of lesson 1.
2. Pray for God's wisdom and guidance in fostering the spiritual development of those in your Bible study group.
3. If you plan to use the *alternate introduction* and the *optional activity*, collect a variety of aftershaves or colognes to use during the group meeting. Also take your favorite cologne to the study.

Group Participation:
1. What are some of your favorite smells? Why do you like them? What smells make you turn your nose away? How would you describe a "good" smell vs. a "bad" smell?
Alternate Introduction: After everyone is seated, and the study is ready to begin, excuse yourself, go into another room and *generously* apply your favorite cologne. Reenter the room, walk within smelling distance of each group member, then sit down. Ask: "Did anyone notice anything in particular about me?" If you have applied your cologne heavily enough, someone is sure to mention it. Then say: "Just as the fragrance we wear on the outside is noticeable to others, so is our inner fragrance. Today we are going to concentrate on the inner fragrance that comes from within us and spills out to others."
Read aloud 2 Corinthians 2:14-16.
2. What "fragrance" do Paul and the Corinthians wear? How do you think this kind of fragrance got noticed by those around them?
3. Are you conscious of being a distributor of the aroma of Christ? How do you think others, both Christians and unbelievers, perceive you? What are some things that might be spoiling your fragrance?
Optional Activity: Distribute the variety of colognes or aftershaves you have collected. Ask group members to smell each one. Discuss likes and dislikes. Point out how the same cologne can have different appeal.
4. In 2 Corinthians 2:15-16, Paul speaks of two different responses to Christians. Why do you think there are different reactions to the fragrance of Christ? What are some ways that a Christian can affect that reaction?

5. Read John 3:16-21. In view of these words, what does it mean to be "saved"? According to this passage, how is a person saved, and who can be saved?
6. Paul says in his metaphor about fragrance that some will "perish" because they do not follow Christ (v. 15). Who do you worry about because you fear that they do not know Christ and are therefore perishing? What are some ways you can be the aroma of Christ to one of these people?

Read aloud 2 Corinthians 2:17.

7. What are some contemporary examples of people "peddling" the Gospel? Why is sincerity so important to spreading the fragrance of Christ? Examine your own motives for sharing the Gospel with others. What are some of your reasons for sharing your faith?
8. Make sure each group member understands how to keep the *Life Action Diary* and how to write her *Pen and Paper Prayer*. If necessary, review the instructions in the *Introduction* or offer individual help after your group meeting.
9. Invite people to talk about additional prayer needs and record them in the *Growing Intimate* section.
10. Close by sharing the *Pen and Paper Prayer* you have each written for this lesson.

❧ GROUP STUDY 2 ❧

Objective:
To help group members understand what it means to be a living letter for Christ; to challenge each other to fulfill our responsibility to create other living letters.

Leader Preparation:
1. Complete and read all parts of lesson 2.
2. Pray for the confidence and competency to lead this lesson. Pray also that God will prepare the hearts of each group member to receive the truths of this lesson.
3. If possible, go to a Christian bookstore, and buy copies of Campus Crusade's tract "The Four Spiritual Laws" so that you can give one to each group member.
4. Bring enough 3 x 5 cards, stationery, and envelopes for each group member.
5. Cut from construction paper enough three-inch hearts that each group member can be given one.
6. Try to obtain some worn and aged letters to use as an object lesson.

Group Participation:
1. Begin with prayer, asking for God's guidance as you study His Word.
Read aloud 2 Corinthians 3:1-6.
2. What does it mean to be a "living letter"?
3. Take a 3 x 5 card and write the names of three people you have had contact with today.
4. How were you a "living letter" to each of these people? Write down next to each name what you think each one "read" in you today (joy, love, anger, impatience, etc.).
5. In a moment of silent prayer, thank God if your messages pointed toward Him. Ask forgiveness if your messages gave a negative picture of Christ and His people.
6. What fruit of the Spirit or character qualities would you like God to make "legible" in your life?
7. Take a moment to pray again, asking God to nurture these qualities in you.
8. According to 2 Corinthians 3:1-6, who is the author of "living letters"?
9. Examine some old, worn letters. What changes have taken place in

the paper and ink? What differences do you see between these old letters and the work of the Holy Spirit as described in Paul's metaphor about living letters?

10. Take a piece of stationery and an envelope. In five minutes, write a brief but "heartfelt" note of thanks to a person who helped you become a living letter for Christ.

11. Using a paper heart and a copy of "The Four Spiritual Laws," write on the heart the name of someone that you would like to see become a living letter for Christ. Take the heart with you and put it where it will remind you to pray daily for the salvation of this person. Consider mailing or giving the booklet to this person along with a personal note explaining your own response to the concepts there and a willingness to discuss it further with your friend.

12. In view of your study this week, how would you summarize the difference between the Old Covenant and the New?

13. Why is the New Covenant "better" than the Old one?

14. Read Galatians 3:19-29. What was the purpose of the Law?

15. In what areas do you see yourself living according to the Old Covenant of laws? How would a deeper appreciation for God's grace change you in those areas?

16. Look again at 2 Corinthians 3:4-6. Where does your confidence and sense of adequacy come from? How has this lesson helped you understand how God Himself equips you to serve Him?

17. Read aloud one entry from your *Life Action Diary* and listen to entries of other people in your group.

18. Record prayer interests of people in your group in the *Growing Intimate* section of your guide, then pray together for these needs.

19. Read to others in your group a *Pen and Paper Prayer* that you wrote for lesson 1 and listen to their prayers.

❦ GROUP STUDY 3 ❦

Objective:
To help group members understand the superiority of the New Covenant so that they can become more effective ministers of it.

Leader Preparation:
1. Complete all parts of lesson 3.
2. Obtain a large picture of the tabernacle (Exodus 26) or have a smaller copy available for each individual.
3. Reread Hebrews 9. Review your answer to questions 6, 9, 10, and 12 in *Gathering Information* of chapter 2. Be prepared to explain the differences between the Old and New Covenants, concentrating on blood sacrifices, priests, the high priest, the veil, and the holy of holies.
4. Pray for the members of your group as they complete this lesson. It may be more challenging than the first two.
5. Obtain a cracked mirror, a dirty mirror, and a magnifying mirror to take to your group session.

Group Participation
1. Have you ever replaced a well-loved object with something new and better? What happened, and how did you feel about the process?
Read aloud 2 Corinthians 3:7-18.
2. When have you experienced something so life-changing that others could see a difference in you? What happened to you, and why did it leave a "visible" impression on you?
3. When God spoke to Moses on Mt. Sinai, Moses' face radiated with the glory of God. But it soon faded. How does this symbolize the insufficiency of the Old Covenant? Why wasn't the Old Covenant enough?
4. What are the three contrasting features of the Old and New Covenants mentioned in verses 7-11? How would you sum up the superiority of the New Covenant?
5. What do you think Paul means by "veiled" faces? Hearts? Minds? Gospel?
6. How was your own "veil" removed by Christ?
   Who, according to Paul, is to clearly reflect Christ's glory?
7. Take a look at yourself in a cracked mirror, a dirty mirror, and then a magnifying mirror. Describe what you see.
8. What "cracks," "dirt," or "magnifiers" in our lives could distort the

glory of God? What can we do about them?

9. What conditions in our lives cause Christ's radiance within us to fade? To increase?

10. Do you think that there are situations today in which a Christian should "veil" her relationship with the Lord? Explain.

11. Paul says that in Christ there is "freedom" (2 Corinthians 3:17). What are we freed from and for what purpose? (You may want to refer also to Romans 6:17-23.)

Read aloud 2 Corinthians 4:1-6.

12. Paul warns us that some people will reject the Gospel we present but that this should not happen because of our methods (4:2-3). What are some ways you have seen people "distort" the Gospel? Are there ways in which you could be more careful about the way you present Christ to others? Explain.

13. Who do you know who is living in darkness? How can you reflect the light of Christ to them this week? Commit one of these people to the Lord in prayer.

14. Read aloud an entry from your *Life-Action Diary* that was particularly meaningful to you this week. Listen thoughtfully to entries from other group members.

15. Record prayer needs of people in your group in your *Growing Intimate* section. Jot today's date by any previous requests that have been answered. Take time to praise God.

16. Close today's session by reading your *Pen and Paper Prayer* for this week's lesson and listening to the penciled prayers of others in your group.

◖ GROUP STUDY 4 ◗

Objective:
To help group members perceive themselves as fragile vessels which display the power of the Gospel to others through their very weakness.

Leader Preparation:
1. Complete all parts of lesson 4.
2. Pray for God's guidance, as you prepare and lead this lesson.
3. Call any group members who might need encouragement.
4. Find two pieces of simple clay pottery to take to your group meeting. One should show signs of use, such as nicks and chips. The other should look new and hardly used.
5. Select a fancy piece of crystal or china and two gold bracelets or necklaces to bring to the meeting.

Group Participation:
1. Compare a fancy piece of crystal or china with a new but simple piece of pottery. What similarities and differences do you find? Lay gold bracelets over the edge of each container. Which vessel allows the beauty of the bracelet to be noticed more? Why? Today we will be studying a treasure far more precious than gold and the unique way the Lord has chosen to display it.

Read aloud 2 Corinthians 4:7-18.
2. What "treasure" is Paul referring to in verse 7? What do the "jars of clay" represent?
3. Compare a piece of new pottery with one that has seen hard use. Which is most like you? Why and how?
4. How would you describe the limitations of clay pottery? Why do you think God has chosen to put His treasure in clay jars?
5. In verse 10, Paul says we display the death of Jesus so that His life may also be made evident. What does Paul mean?
6. What can you do (or be) that will show your own identity with the death of Christ in a way that others can see?
7. When have you been drawn closer to Christ because of someone else's suffering?
8. How do you hope God will use your own suffering to display His power to others? Explain.
9. Paul says in 2 Corinthians 4:13 that we "believe and therefore speak." What could you do to become a better *spokeswoman* for Christ?

10. Look more carefully at 2 Corinthians 4:13-18. What reasons does Paul have to feel discouraged?
11. In spite of these, why is he actually encouraged? (Find answers throughout the text.)
12. What encouragement for yourself do you find in this text? Explain.
13. In view of the sufferings Paul described in 2 Corinthians 4:7-12, why do you think he refers to them as "light and momentary" in verse 17?
14. What aspects of your earthly life do you look forward to being transformed in heaven? How do you imagine them to be changed?
15. Paul invites us in verse 18 to "fix our eyes . . . on what is unseen." What are some specific ways that you can attempt that this week?
16. Share an entry from your *Life Action Diary* and listen to the writings of others in your group.
17. Record prayer concerns of people in your group in your *Growing Intimate* section; then pray together about these concerns.
18. Read together several *Pen and Paper Prayers.*

◖ *GROUP STUDY 5* ◖

Objective:
To provide hope for group members regarding death.

Leader Preparation:
1. Complete all parts of lesson 5.
2. Write a short note to each group member to let her know you appreciate her being a part of the group.
3. Pray for each member of the group.

Group Participation:
1. Have ever slept overnight in a tent? What happened?
2. Would you recommend a tent as a long-term place to live? Why or why not?

Read aloud 2 Corinthians 5:1-4.
3. When Paul talks about our "earthly tent" what is he referring to? What is he saying with this word picture?
4. How would you compare your earthly body to your heavenly one? (You may want to refer also to 1 Corinthians 15:35-44.)

Read aloud 2 Corinthians 5:5-10.
5. Confident of his heavenly body to come, Paul longed to be clothed with it. Do you long for heaven? Explain.
6. There is a sense in Paul's writings that if we are "away from the Lord" it is to accomplish something for God on earth. To what extent is your "goal" (verse 9) to please God while you are here? Explain.
7. What areas of your life would you like to make more pleasing to God?
8. How can Paul's words in 1 Corinthians 5:1-10 bring comfort to you or someone you know who is suffering or facing death? (Find specific phrases from the text that could help ease your fears about some current or potential event.)
9. Have you ever been afraid to die? Are you afraid now? Explain.

Read aloud Revelation 21 and 22.
10. What descriptions here of heaven are especially meaningful to you? Give some reasons why.
11. Leader: Ask for two volunteers to role play a five-minute conversation where one person is a Christian and the other is an unbeliever facing death. Afterward, discuss what was helpful and comforting as well as what could have been handled differently.

12. Record in the *Growing Intimate* section current prayer requests from your group. Also record together answers God has granted to your previous united prayers.
13. Read a section of journaling in your *Life-Action Diary*. Listen to the journal entries of other group members.
14. Close the study by reading several *Pen and Paper Prayers*.

❧ GROUP STUDY GUIDE 6 ❧

Objective:
To help group members appreciate God's protective principle of not entering into binding relationships with unbelievers.

Leader Preparation:
1. Complete all sections of lesson 6.
2. Pray for God's guidance as you lead this lesson. Be sensitive to the possibility that some group members may already be in a marriage or other binding relationship with an unbeliever. The purpose of this lesson is not to place group members under condemnation for already established relationships but to appreciate the intent of God's command regarding binding relationships and to obey it in the future.
3. Obtain a copy of *Beloved Unbeliever: Loving Your Husband into the Faith* by Jo Berry (Zondervan, 1981). This book will prove a reassuring help to any group member who wishes to borrow it.

Group Participation:
1. If you were looking for a business partner, what kind of person would you be looking for? Why?
2. What do you know about yourself that would help you choose a partner for a sports team? A close friendship?
Read 2 Corinthians 6:14–7:1.
3. What, according to this passage, does God know about Christians that would help them choose partners?
4. What are some general areas of disagreement between Christians and unbelievers?
5. What hardships have you experienced because of a close relationship with someone who did not believe as you do?
6. In what ways have you sensed God's kindness to you, even in spite of these hardships?
7. Some of our "yokes" are already part of our family relationships. Read 1 Corinthians 7:12-16. What is a Christian in this situation to do and not do? Why?
8. If you were in a family that contained unbelievers, what comfort and support do you find in this passage?
9. Not all relationships are "yokes." Read 1 Corinthians 9:19-23 and 1 Corinthians 10:27. What principles here would help you make decisions about what to join and not join?

10. Look again at 2 Corinthians 6:16-18. What do you appreciate about the relationship described here?
11. Verse 16 says that you are God's "temple." What does this mean? (See also 1 Corinthians 3:16-19 and 6:15-20.)
12. What are some practical ways that you can live out the concept of "temple"? (Consider your relationships with other believers and also what you do with your own body.)
13. Where is your "temple" in need of repair?
14. Look more carefully at 2 Corinthians 7:1. Paul says that we are to be "perfecting holiness." Why and how?
15. What practices contaminate our bodies? Our spirits?
16. What is one step that you can take to better express your reverence for God?
17. Share entries from several *Life Action Diaries.*
18. Record ideas for prayer in your *Growing Intimate* section.
19. Close by reading several *Pen and Paper Prayers.*

❦ LEADER'S GUIDE 7 ❦

Objective:
To motivate each other to give generously, cheerfully, and creatively to God and to others.

Leader Preparation:
1. Complete all parts of lesson 7.
2. If possible, obtain a copy of the poem, "Children Learn What They Live" (usually available in a Christian bookstore).
3. Pray for each member of the group.

Group Participation:
1. Read "Children Learn What They Live." What memories does this poem bring to your mind?
   Discuss briefly the sowing and reaping of attitudes and actions reflected in this poem.
2. How would you express the idea behind this poem in a single sentence?
   Note: If you are unable to obtain this poem discuss question 1 on page 59.

Read aloud 2 Corinthians 9:6-15.
3. What words and phrases here encourage people to give and also to receive gifts?
4. What principles in these verses would help you decide how to give and how much to give? (Find something in each verse.)
5. What relationship can you see between the farmer's work as it is described here and the act of giving?
6. Verse 6 says that we are to give generously. What (besides money) could be involved in generous giving?
7. What are some creative ways that a woman, who has little income of her own, could participate in the kind of giving described in verses 6-7?
8. According to verses 8-11, how does God reward the person who gives generously?
9. How have you experienced the kinds of rewards described here?
10. Reread 2 Corinthians 9:12-15. What reasons (other than personal reward) does Paul cite here for generous giving?
11. What effect does generous giving have on relationships among God's people?
12. Several times in this passage Paul tells us that our own generous

giving to meet each other's needs results in thanks and praise to God. Why is this appropriate?

13. When have you seen God's work accomplished through the gifts of His people?

14. Read 2 Corinthians 8:9 and Philippians 4:19. How is the idea of wealth, as it is presented here and in 2 Corinthians 9, different from the normal worldview?

15. Read Mark 12:41-44. Why might it be hard for a poor person to give?

16. Read Matthew 19:21-26. Why might it be difficult for a rich person to give?

17. When you do not give as generously as you think you ought, what excuses do you offer yourself?

18. Paul closes his remarks about sowing and reaping by speaking of God's "indescribable gift." Who and what is that gift? (See John 3:16-18 if you need more information.)

19. How does God's own gift illustrate the kind of giving taught in 2 Corinthians 9?

20. On a scale of 1 to 10, how well do you think you are doing in following these biblical teachings about giving? (Consider time, money, shared resources, etc.)

21. If you cannot honestly give yourself a "10," what is one way in which you could better follow these teachings?

22. Record prayer interests in your *Growing Intimate* section. Discuss and record answers to prayers.

23. Read entries to each other from *Life Action Diaries*.

24. End the lesson by reading several *Pen and Paper Prayers*.

❧ GROUP STUDY GUIDE 8 ❧

Objective:
To realize the great value of our weaknesses and suffering.

Leader Preparation:
1. Complete all sections of lesson 8. If you are able, read various commentaries to see what speculations have been made concerning Paul's "thorn," so that you can share them with the members of the group.
2. Since this is the last lesson, you may wish to plan something special such as refreshments or a pitch-in lunch or dinner.
3. Pray for the needs of each person in the group.

Group Participation:
1. What it is like to have a splinter or thorn embedded in your flesh, and what would it be like to live with it, if it could not be removed? NOTE: *Paul had an affliction which he called a "thorn in the flesh." No one knows for sure what his thorn was, but it caused him anguish. We will see in today's lesson how that thorn, which could have caused Paul to be bitter against God, instead kept Paul humble before God.*
Read aloud 2 Corinthians 12:1-6.
2. Paul says in verse 2 that he was taken to the third heaven. In view of the way he described that event, what do you think he heard and saw there?
3. Why do you think Paul described his supernatural experience as if it happened to someone else? Why do you think he waited fourteen years?
4. What do Paul's statements in the passage suggest about his motives for telling about his experience?
5. Do you think people still receive visions from God? Why or why not?
6. Paul began in verse 1 by saying that he was boasting. Why? (You may want to review information in 1 Corinthians 11.)
7. Of what value might this story of Paul's experience be to the Corinthians?
8. In what situations today might a woman of God need to boast because of motives similar to Paul's?
Read aloud 2 Corinthians 12:7-9.
9. In what different ways did Paul react to his "thorn in the flesh"?
10. What reason does Paul give for why God did not take away his "thorn"?

11. What did Paul gain from enduring his suffering?
12. What do you consider to be your own "thorn in the flesh"?
13. What have been some of your responses to your thorn?
14. In what ways have you experienced God's strength because of your own weakness?
15. What has your thorn led you to turn over to God?
16. Select one of the passages below and explain how it might help you as you endure your personal thorn.

    Isaiah 40:28-31
    Isaiah 41:10
    Romans 8:35-39
    Ephesians 3:14-19
    Philippians 4:11-13
    Hebrews 12:5-6

17. Why is it important for us to remember that God sets the limits on how much suffering we endure—as in the case of Job?
18. What would you like your believing friends to ask God for you as you continue to endure a "thorn" that will not go away?
19. Read to each other meaningful entries from your *Life Action Diaries.*
20. Share prayer requests and answers, and record them in the *Growing Intimate* section.
21. Share how the *Growing Intimate* section has been meaningful to you.
22. Close your study by praying together.

Introduction
1. Gary Smalley and John Trent, *The Language of Love* (Pomona, California: Focus on the Family Publishing, 1988), p. 17.

Chapter 2
1. Charles Swindoll, *Steadfast Christianity* (Fullerton, California: Insight for Living, 1986), p. 51.
2. Ibid., p. 50.
3. D. James Kennedy, *Evangelism Explosion* (Wheaton, Illinois: Tyndale House Publishers, 1977), p. 26.
4. Ibid., p. 27.

Chapter 4
1. Roy L. Laurin, *Second Corinthians: Where Life Endures* (Grand Rapids, Michigan: Kregel Publications, 1985), p. 83.

✳✳ Notes ✳✳

✲✲ Notes ✲✲

✳✳ Notes ✳✳

*** Notes ***

✹✹ Notes ✹✹

⁂ Notes ⁂

✳✳ Notes ✳✳